STRATEGIC RETHINK

FRIENDS, FOES, AND FUTURE DIRECTIONS

U.S. Partnerships in a Turbulent World

T0306708

Hans Binnendijk

RAND CORPORATION

For more information on this publication, visit www.rand.org/t/RR1210

Library of Congress Cataloging-in-Publication Data is available for this publication.
ISBN: 978-0-8330-9220-5

Published by the RAND Corporation, Santa Monica, Calif.

Preface

This report is the third in a series of volumes in which RAND explores the elements of a national strategy for the conduct of U.S. foreign policy in a fast-changing world. The initial volume in this Strategic Rethink series, *Choices for America in a Turbulent World*, examined the most critical decisions the next president is likely to face, and thus likely to be debated during the 2016 election campaign. It covered two global issues, climate change and the world economy; assessed potential directions for national defense; evaluated issues related to counterterrorism and cybersecurity; and explored U.S. strategic choices in three key regions, Europe, the Middle East and South Asia, and East Asia.

The subsequent studies in this series take up where the initial volume left off and examine in more detail a range of long-term policy issues and organizational, financial, and diplomatic challenges that will confront senior U.S. officials now, in 2017, and beyond, including national defense, institutional reform of the U.S. system for managing national security, reducing strategic surprise, and the global economy.

This volume focuses on U.S. friends and potential foes, and analyzes how alliances and partnerships may evolve to meet the diverse potential challenges to regional and global security. It considers the degree to which the United States wishes to be assertive, to collaborate, or to retrench, given the demands of the emerging strategic environment.

This volume should be of interest to defense and foreign policy decisionmakers in the United States and allied nations, analysts, the media, the staff and advisers to the 2016 presidential candidates, nongovernmental organizations, and others concerned about the role of the United States and other nations in advancing global security.

This project results from the RAND Corporation's Investment in People and Ideas program. Support for this program is provided, in part, by philanthropic contributions from donors and by the independent research and development provisions of RAND's contracts for the operation of its U.S. Department of Defense federally funded research and development centers. Special appreciation goes to the Hauser Foundation for its generous gift in support of the project and to Rita Hauser for encouraging RAND to undertake it.

For more information on the International Security and Defense Policy Center, see www.rand.org/nsrd/ndri/centers/isdp or contact the director (contact information is provided on the web page).

Contents

Figures and Tables

Figures

Tables

Executive Summary

Today, the most important external challenge faced by the United States is the reemergence of potential confrontation between great powers and with rogue states. The United States now faces a risk of conflict with several potential adversaries: Four are nation-states with nuclear weapons or nuclear ambitions (Russia, China, North Korea, and Iran) and one is a diverse group of Salafi jihadists. Currently, the United States is engaged in military action against a wannabe state, the Islamic State of Iraq and Syria (ISIS).[1] Most of these potential adversaries also cooperate with at least one other hostile nation, compounding the challenge for the United States.

This is a fundamental change from the previous decade, when the focus of U.S. national security policy was on two stability operations in the greater Middle East, nonstate actors, and transnational threats. Those threats still exist, but a new set of challenges from nuclear states and nuclear aspirants is of greater concern.

There are dramatic differences among these potential adversaries in terms of their ability to threaten vital U.S. interests and the extent to which their goals overlap with Washington's. As a result, the United States must design a set of flexible and differentiated policies to deal

---

[1] The organization's name transliterates from Arabic as *al-Dawlah al-Islamiyah fi al-'Iraq wa al-Sham* (abbreviated as Da'ish or DAESH). In the West, it is commonly referred to as the Islamic State of Iraq and the Levant (ISIL), the Islamic State of Iraq and Syria, the Islamic State of Iraq and the Sham (both abbreviated as ISIS), or simply as the Islamic State (IS). Arguments abound as to which is the most accurate translation, but here we refer to the group as ISIS.

with each potential foe. The overall goal should be to reduce these threats and the prospect of close cooperation among adversaries to challenge U.S. interests. To do this, the United States needs to quickly defeat ISIS, deter North Korea, dissuade Russia, constrain Iran, and engage China.

These potential adversaries have created situations in which a large number of U.S. allies and partner nations are more vulnerable today than they were a decade ago. Many U.S. friends are in more danger than the United States is itself, and if the United States should be drawn into conflict with any of these adversaries (as it has already been drawn into conflict with ISIS), it will probably be to defend its partners more than itself. The principal risk to the United States is that conflicts with any of these adversaries could escalate. Involvement by the three nuclear powers (Russia, China, or—to a lesser degree—North Korea) could pose existential risks.

While its partners remain a major U.S. asset that its adversaries do not enjoy to the same degree, many of those partnerships do present problems. Many partners are only slowly waking up to these changing international circumstances and have not yet taken up an adequate share of the global defense burden. Some partners do not fully share many of the United States' values or interests and require flexibility in the relationship. And the most-vulnerable partners will need to work more closely with the United States to coordinate policies and crisis-management plans in advance so that the United States will not be drawn into unforeseen conflict against its will.

As the United States prepares to deal with adversaries and to help defend partners, it is at risk of becoming overextended. U.S. national security resources are shrinking as its challenges are expanding. U.S. engagement with friends and foes alike, therefore, must reconcile this potential mismatch between resources and requirements, and between means and ends.

To mitigate this mismatch, U.S. policymakers have at least three general approaches to consider:

- First, the United States could take an assertive approach focused primarily on American values, thereby limiting compromise with potential adversaries. Washington would seek a few capable partners but would be prepared to go it alone or with a small coalition of the willing if needed. This "assertive engagement" option would require a significant increase in defense spending.

- Second, the United States could seek greater defense contributions from allies and partners. Under such a policy, termed "collaborative engagement," the United States would act based primarily on its interests and would seek to further harmonize its policies more with its major allies and strategic partners. It would be more dependent on the will of its partners and would be inclined to seek some accommodation, where possible, with potential adversaries. It would be more restrained in its policy choices and stress regional trade partnerships.
- Third, the United States could reduce its ambitions and focus on only the most critical challenges to its own vital national interests. In some cases, it might need to reduce its commitments to partners. It would stress homeland resilience and seek to find surrogates to take the lead wherever possible. This alternative is called "retrenchment."

All three alternatives are constrained by external factors. Assertive engagement is constrained by the current U.S. defense budget, military posture (as described in the most recent Quadrennial Defense Review), and the reluctance of the American people to engage in large military operations again. One U.S. election is unlikely to fundamentally change those constraints. It would probably take another direct attack on the homeland, like 9/11, to shift both public opinion and spending priorities enough to finance this approach.

Retrenched engagement is constrained by the number and nature of potential adversaries ready to confront the United States. Given today's foes, retrenchment will be difficult to implement. The United States would need to be prepared to make significant concessions to adversaries and to adjust commitments to partners, possibly undermining the credibility of their military deterrent. It could stimulate adversaries to take advantage of the opportunity. Allies may react to a reduction in perceived protection from the United States by seeking their own nuclear deterrent or fueling a conventional arms race.

Collaborative engagement is constrained by the will and capabilities of U.S. partners. Washington has championed greater burden-sharing for decades, yet today its allies are—for varying reasons—either less capable or less well organized than the United States would like. Can this change? New threats from potential adversaries have created anxiety among U.S. regional partners that could be converted into greater burden-sharing. Managed properly, greater collaboration can work.

In establishing regional strategies, Washington may need to draw on elements of all three approaches. Europe is well organized institutionally, but has lived for two and a half decades with a sense of low military threat and, since 2008, with economic crisis. There are also deep divisions within Europe on both security and economic matters, as the recent migration crisis has demonstrated. Several nations are militarily exhausted by the North Atlantic Treaty Organization's (NATO's) mission in Afghanistan. As a result, European military capabilities have declined markedly. The two strongest allies in Europe, the United Kingdom and France, are also overextended, albeit for different reasons. It would be difficult for European allies alone to mount a major joint military operation—including defense of the Baltic states—without the United States. Therefore, the United States will need to maintain a significant force structure in Europe capable of both rapid reaction and providing military enablers for its allies. This requirement creates tension with the U.S. desire to encourage its European partners to contribute more to the common defense, since many feel they can rely on the United States without increasing defense spending.

NATO has been able to mitigate some of this tension by operating flexibly and creating efficiencies, called "smart defense," and the framework nation concept. But the impact of these efficiency measures is limited. Russian aggression in Ukraine has so far forged greater unity within NATO, as evidenced by the 2014 Wales Summit defense spending pledge and by agreement to impose sanctions against Russia. Implementing the Wales Summit communiqué will pose difficulties for European partners, and the United States may need to take a firmer stance in pressing its European allies to live up to their commitments. Chapter Five contains multiple suggestions for overcoming this tension. Germany's rising leadership role, Turkey's Islamic drift, and Britain's potential divorce from the European Union make them three of the most pivotal countries in Europe. Their future direction will profoundly affect the future of the transatlantic relationship. In addition, even as NATO increases its defense capabilities in response to Russian aggression, the United States will also wish to keep Europe engaged in Middle Eastern crisis management operations and in engaging Asia. Russian President Vladimir Putin's behavior therefore creates some prospect that collaborative engagement could work in Europe.

Asia is facing an arms race, but starting from a lower base than Europe. The three strongest U.S. partners in Asia today are Japan, South Korea, and Australia. India is also a potentially important partner that can help stabilize the region. Most of China's neighbors are feeling more vulnerable to potential Chinese aggression and are seeking closer security ties with the United States for protection. China is also the major trading partner for most of these vulnerable nations. Under Prime Minister Shinzo Abe, Japan has increased its defense spending, reinterpreted its constitution to allow it to perform a wider regional defense role, and developed new defense guidelines with the United States to that end. This response to Chinese policies also provides some potential for greater collaborative engagement in Asia as well.

The greatest weakness in the U.S. posture in Asia is the lack of strong collaborative security institutions. U.S. security arrangements in the region are bilateral. There is nothing in Asia like NATO, with its high degree of military interoperability and political consultation. And there are no strong regional institutions comparable to the European Union or the Organization for Security and Cooperation in Europe. For collaborative engagement to work in Asia, the United States would need to encourage a much-higher degree of multilateral military cooperation among its principal Asian allies, especially Japan and South Korea. This would require strengthening the security institutions of the Association of Southeast Asian Nations as well. In the interim—and given this weak security architecture—the United States cannot retrench in Asia. It should seek to reorganize Asian security in such a way that China does not interpret it as containment, a very difficult task. Efforts to strengthen trade and financial ties with China and to seek a solution to the South and East China seas maritime claims issues are critical to managing the U.S. relationship with China. Japan and India are the two pivotal partners in Asia. For collaborative engagement to succeed in the long run, the United States would need to pay special attention to both.

The Middle East presents a much more complicated partnership problem than does Europe or Asia. During the George W. Bush administration, the U.S. posture in the region was assertive; more recently, the United States has shown greater restraint. Neither posture has worked particularly well. The four most important traditional U.S. allies in the greater Middle East (Israel, Egypt, Saudi Arabia, and Pakistan) today have difficult relations with the United States. Further, there are ongoing civil wars in at least five countries where the United States has either directly or indirectly supported regime change (Iraq, Afghanistan, Libya, Yemen, and Syria). The Syrian civil war in particular risks creating even greater regional sectarian conflict. Because of this turmoil, the expansion of Salafi terrorist activity, and the growth in Iranian influence, U.S. partners throughout the region are more vulnerable than they were a few years ago. Strategic tools used historically by the United States do not appear to work well in the Middle East.

Yet two recent opportunities create some hope that a version of collective engagement might succeed. First, the United States has been able to rally many Sunni nations to join the coalition against ISIS. Second, the nuclear deal with Iran offers an opportunity to improve overall relations with Tehran. If the United States can accomplish the difficult task of rebuilding its ties with traditional allies (by strengthening their militaries and, on occasion, postponing judgment on their values) as it creates a new relationship with Shi'ite Iran, a new approach could yet be designed for the Middle East.

None of the three alternative approaches analyzed here is ideal. All are constrained. A hybrid approach will be needed. But of the three, collaborative engagement is the most attractive and potentially viable strategy. Its purpose would be to harmonize U.S. goals and national security resources by placing a greater burden on partners and allies without retrenching from global interests. It would also seek to reduce the risk of greater collusion among potential U.S. adversaries. Its implementation would need to be crafted carefully and flexibly, with regard to both managing potential adversaries and strengthening regional partners. In the case of both Russia and China, getting this balance right will be quite difficult. However, the United States was able to manage a similar policy with the Soviet Union during the Cold War.

Implementation would include policies and programs designed to

- improve relations with China and Iran
- defeat ISIS and continue targeted attacks against al Qaeda
- deter North Korea
- dissuade Russia from aggression
- enhance military capabilities and political will in NATO
- strengthen security institutions in Asia
- develop stronger trilateral relations to connect our European and Asian allies
- rebuild ties with traditional allies in the Middle East
- develop military capabilities of potential coalition partners
- provide security-sector support to and coordinate policies with vulnerable partners.

If properly managed, this collaborative approach could yield a "new trilateralism" that might encompass the pivot to Asia, reinforce transatlantic ties, and provide greater partner support to manage instability in the Middle East.

Acknowledgments

This paper is part of a project on U.S. grand strategy initiated by Richard Solomon. Solomon held numerous conversations with the author and provided excellent general guidance for this study. Andrew Hoehn oversaw RAND's overall effort on grand strategy and also provided useful comments for this study. James Dobbins managed the production of the series and viewed several draft versions. Seth Jones read two drafts of the paper and provided several critical structural suggestions. Sonni Efron was the general editor for the series and provided extensive editorial improvements. Laura Baldwin also made several useful comments. Bryce Schoenborn provided final editorial suggestions. Together, this RAND team helped shape the study through multiple drafts.

Five RAND reviewers provided quality assurance, and each made the subsequent paper a more accurate and focused product. These reviewers were David Gompert, Stephen Larrabee, Michael Mazarr, Andrew Liepman, and Michael Chase. In addition, several analysts contributed to the study by providing memos, reading drafts, or hosting workshops. They include Andrew Weiss, Dalia Dassa Kaye, Peter Wilson, and Eric Heginbotham. Finally, Zack Steinborn and Joy Merck provided great assistance in managing draft products.

The author is grateful to each of those named above for their role in shaping and improving this study. However, the analysis and conclusions contained in this study are those of the author alone.

CHAPTER ONE

Introduction

This report focuses primarily on the U.S. relationship with its potential adversaries and partners and is based solely on unclassified material. The assessment presented here relies primarily on a qualitative analysis of U.S. friends and potential foes based on extensive research; interviews in the United States, Europe, and Japan; multiple expert workshops at RAND and elsewhere; and four decades of personal experience in dealing with U.S. partners. It reviews the nature of the challenges posed by potential adversaries, both individually and as a whole, and suggests a general approach to how the United States might respond. It also analyzes the ways in which these and other challenges have affected U.S. partnerships, by creating more-vulnerable allies and what might be called pivotal partners. It also suggests ways in which the United States might strengthen its partnerships and address the so-called free-rider problem.[1]

This study considers how the U.S. perception of its role in the world—to be assertive, to collaborate, or to retrench—will affect relationships with friends and foes. Each of these potential approaches is represented in today's American body politic. The United States might want to pursue assertive policies and be the dominant leader. Alternatively, it might retrench and let others lead. Or, the United States might

[1] The free-rider problem refers to a situation in which those who benefit from the provision of resources, goods, or services do not pay for them, leading to underprovision of those resources. For example, many of the United States' key allies spend well under 2 percent of their gross domestic product (GDP) on defense, while the United States spends well over 4 percent of its GDP to fulfill security commitments to those allies.

seek greater collaboration with its allies and give them a larger share of the burden.

In analyzing these three general approaches, this study suggests three tests. Retrenchment is judged primarily by the nature of the challenges presented by adversaries. How far can the United States retrench in the face of committed adversaries? Assertiveness is judged by budgetary and public opinion constraints. To what degree can the United States sustain an assertive posture, given the reality of today's defense budgets and public will to act? Collaboration is judged by the willingness and capability of partners to share a greater security burden. Can the United States be truly collaborative if most of its closest partners underinvest in defense?

This analysis further recognizes that security situations are markedly different from region to region; thus, the report dedicates one chapter each to three key regions of the world—Europe, Asia, and the Middle East—and seeks to suggest possible regional strategies for the United States and its partners.

Whereas nonstate actors have become increasingly important in today's international environment, this study concentrates primarily on state actors, including aspirational states like the Islamic State of Iraq and Syria (ISIS).[2] This is because the challenges to U.S. interests from state actors have returned and become much more dangerous in recent years. The focus on Europe, Asia, and the Middle East is not because Latin America and sub-Saharan Africa are not important, but because the security threats to the United States emanating from those two regions are relatively less critical.

---

[2] The organization's name transliterates from Arabic as *al-Dawlah al-Islamiyah fi al-'Iraq wa al-Sham* (abbreviated as Da'ish or DAESH). In the West, it is commonly referred to as the Islamic State of Iraq and the Levant (ISIL), the Islamic State of Iraq and Syria, the Islamic State of Iraq and the Sham (both abbreviated as ISIS), or simply as the Islamic State (IS). Arguments abound as to which is the most accurate translation, but here we refer to the group as ISIS.

CHAPTER TWO

The Partnership Setting

The Historical Importance of U.S. Partnerships

To achieve its strategic goals, the United States relies heavily on its allies and coalition partners—the "outer defenses" of America's security system. It needs partners around the world to help anchor the array of international diplomatic, security, and economic institutions created over the past 70 years to provide a degree of global order. It depends on partners for trade, investment, economic growth, freedom of travel, and a rules-based international financial system. Partners help protect shared liberal democratic values. The United States relies on partners for legitimacy and intelligence cooperation, and for an array of mutual defense treaties and security arrangements that allow the U.S. military to operate globally.

U.S. partners have often been partners in arms. The United States seldom fights alone. During the First World War, the United States joined the Triple Entente, but the total number of allies numbered at least a dozen, plus many colonies. During the Second World War, the allies included some 23 nations. Since 1945, the approximate numbers of U.S. partners in war have been as follows: the Korean War (27), the Vietnam War (seven in combat plus seven support), Desert Storm (38), Kosovo (18 members of the North Atlantic Treaty Organization [NATO] plus the Kosovo Liberation Army), Multinational Force–Iraq (as high as 49), International Security Assistance Force (ISAF; 27 NATO partners and 22 others), Libya (NATO, with 13 NATO nations in combat, plus Sweden and four Middle Eastern countries). The anti-ISIS coalition includes 59 other nations, as well as the European Union and the Arab League. In recent years, the military contribution of U.S. partners has become relatively smaller but nonetheless important. The numbers not only enhance the international legitimacy of these operations but also buttress support on the U.S. home front. U.S. adversaries are unable to generate anywhere near the same kind of global partnerships or coalitions, a distinct advantage for the United States.

Diplomatically, U.S. partners have formed the backbone of the international organizations and institutions that support a rules-based, well-functioning international system. These include institutions such as the United Nations, the International Monetary Fund, the World Bank, the World Trade Organization, and NATO. Most were formed by the United States and its close allies after the Second World War. Many are in need of adaptation to accommodate the interests of new emerging powers.

Economically, the United States has traditionally relied on relatively free trade to stimulate economic growth at home. The role of the U.S. dollar as the dominant global currency and the power of U.S. direct investment further contribute to American economic strength. Today, the United States is the largest global exporter of commercial services and the second largest exporter of merchandise. Imports and exports together account for 30 percent of U.S. GDP, and exports support some 11.3 million American jobs.[1]

More broadly, the national security strategy of the United States is often defined by partnership relations. Containment was about protecting a group of pro-American partners around the globe from the encroachment of Communism. Enlargement was about creating new democratic partners after the fall of the Soviet Union. Preemption was about protecting the United States and its partners from terrorism by acting in concert to prevent further attacks. And the Obama administration's "pivot" to Asia is about rebalancing the U.S. focus from one group of partners to another.

---

[1] Stephanie Han and Natalie Soraka, *U.S. Trade Overview, 2013*, Washington, D.C.: Department of Commerce, October 2014.

Global Trends Affecting U.S. Partnerships

Global trends will have an important impact on the future U.S. approach to engagement with its partners. A review of ten recent studies reveals eight relevant trends:[2]

- Global power is shifting from Western nations to the east, for economic reasons, and from nation-states to nonstate actors, for technological reasons.
- The liberal international order and its norms are being challenged across the globe, making U.S. partners more vulnerable.
- Ultra-nationalism, religious fanaticism, and political extremism are on the rise and will complicate compromise solutions, particularly in the Middle East.
- The spread of advanced military technology will increasingly enable adversaries to deny the U.S. military access to their neigh-

---

[2] An analysis of global trends was first conducted in 2013 by the author for the Center for Naval Analysis. The studies reviewed are: U.S. National Intelligence Council, *Global Trends 2030: Alternative Worlds*, Washington, D.C.: U.S. Government Printing Office, 2012; Delégation aux Affaires Stratégiques, *Strategic Horizons*, Paris: French Defense Ministry, 2013; Canadian Department of National Defence, *The Future Security Environment 2008–2030,* Part 1: *Current and Emerging Trends*, Ottawa, 2009; UK Ministry of Defence, *Global Strategic Trends—Out to 2040*, 4th ed., London, 2010; U.S. Joint Forces Command, *Joint Operating Environment 2010*, Norfolk, Va.: U.S. Government Printing Office, 2010; European Union Institute for Security Studies, *Global Trends 2030—Citizens in an Interconnected and Polycentric World*, Condé-sur-Noireau, France: Corlet Imprimeur, 2012; QinetiQ, Lloyd's Register, and University of Strathclyde Glasgow, *Global Marine Trends 2030*, London, 2013; North Atlantic Treaty Organization, *Multiple Futures Project: Navigating Towards 2030*, 2009; Barry Pavel and Magnus Nordenman, "Global Trends and the Future of NATO: Alliance Security in an Era of Global Competition," Washington, D.C.: Atlantic Council and Norwegian Institute for Defence Studies, October 2013; Allied Command Transformation, *Strategic Foresight Analysis*, North Atlantic Treaty Organization, April 8, 2013; Daniel Hamilton and Kurt Volker, eds., *Transatlantic 2020: A Tale of Four Futures*, Washington, D.C.: Center for Transatlantic Relations, 2012.

These general trends have recently appeared in two published volumes. For further details see Hans Binnendijk, ed., *A Transatlantic Pivot to Asia: Towards New Trilateral Partnerships*, Washington, D.C.: Center for Transatlantic Relations at Johns Hopkins University, School of Advanced International Studies, 2014, pp. 3–28; and Joint Air Power Competence Center, *Air and Space Power in NATO: Future Vector*—Part 1, Kalkar, Germany: North Atlantic Treaty Organization, July 2014b, pp. 37–62.

borhood, making it more difficult for the United States to come to the aid of its partners.

- The spread of technology is also creating enhanced vulnerabilities, with nuclear proliferation and cyber warfare at the top of the list.
- Climate change, greater urbanization, and the spread of infectious diseases like Ebola will create more humanitarian crises.
- Continued economic inequality and resource scarcity could trigger greater strategic competition; future economic shocks are possible.
- International complexity and information velocity could create more strategic surprises and less time for decisionmaking.

Strategic surprises, by definition, could upend any of these trends or trigger unforeseen interactions among them. For example, the Putin regime in Russia or the Kim regime in North Korea might collapse; growth in the Chinese economy could stall, triggering domestic political disruption; the U.S. effort to defuse nuclear tensions with Iran could fail; ISIS might survive and thrive; the Middle East could become embroiled in a region-wide sectarian war; free trade talks could collapse; NATO unity could be severely damaged or destroyed. The goal of this report, however, is to explore implications for the United States' friends, foes, and future directions in the environment suggested by these current trends.

These eight general trends could create an even more complex and potentially dangerous international environment in which the United States and its partners must operate. This, in turn, suggests four different challenges that might serve as a focal point for U.S. strategy for the next decade:

- A *normative* challenge to the liberal democratic order from several states and quasi-states, including Russia, China, North Korea, Iran, and ISIS, some of which may be partnering more closely together on a bilateral basis.
- A *transnational* challenge from nonstate actors, including weapons of mass destruction in the hands of rogue actors, terrorism,

cybercrime, human trafficking, and criminal cartels, that undermine the writ of some states.
- A broad "responsibility to protect" *humanitarian* challenge driven by new Malthusian trends (increased urbanization, scarce resources), incipient genocide, post-conflict reconstruction, climate change, natural disasters, or pandemics such as Ebola.
- An *international economic* challenge driven by the need to boost domestic economies, avoid possible renewed global recession, and address unequal income distribution.

Elements of a strategy could be designed around each of these four challenges. For example, dealing with those adversaries seeking to overturn the current liberal democratic order might call for a strategy to divide, deter, and (when necessary) defeat them. Transnational threats might be dealt with using a strategy designed to prevent, preempt, and police those threats. Humanitarian crises could lead to a strategy to conserve resources, cooperate to manage crises, and contribute foreign assistance to victimized populations. A focus on international economic challenges could yield a strategy focused on freer trade and greater aid.

In discussing such global challenges, German Chancellor Angela Merkel recently noted: "All of these [challenges] can only be mastered . . . if we act together, if we act in close partnership and coordination with our partners and friends in the United States."[3] That is true for all four of these sets of challenges. This report will focus primarily on the challenge posed to the United States by potential state-based adversaries, the most formidable of the four challenges.

Partnerships Increasingly Require U.S. Political Flexibility

The complex global trends summarized above can interact to make partnerships more dynamic and unstable. In some cases, Washington's

[3] Angela Merkel, "Remarks by Secretary Kerry: Remarks with German Chancellor Angela Merkel Before Their Meeting," Berlin, Germany, U.S. Department of State, October 22, 2014.

best friends show signs of irritation at U.S. policies. In other cases, partners take positions that could push the United States into unwanted conflict. Extreme political positions are taken within alliance structures. Conversely, common interests often draw the United States into working with traditional adversaries. For example,

- Germany is one of the United States' closest European allies and has relied heavily on the United States for security in the past. Yet Germans were infuriated by revelations that the U.S. National Security Agency was spying on German citizens, and Germany walked away from Operation Unified Protector in Libya.
- Israel receives more than $3 billion annually from the United States, but is not influenced by American concerns over its settlements policy and efforts to contend with Iran's nuclear program.
- Turkey is a NATO ally that has hosted U.S. Patriot missiles, but it consistently blocks closer NATO relations with the European Union, has been reluctant to tackle ISIS, and is considering buying Chinese military equipment.
- Japan is a close U.S. ally engaged in a dangerous dispute with China over the Senkaku Islands, but Japan has resisted U.S. admonitions both to pay more attention to the historical sensitivities of its neighbors and to exceed its defense-spending cap, set at 1 percent of GDP.
- Hungary, a member of the NATO alliance, has indicated that the Putin model of government may be more appropriate than the Western model.
- Saudi Arabia is a key U.S. partner in the Middle East, but wealthy Saudis support Wahhabi causes that generate terrorist activity. Saudi Arabia is also conducting an indiscriminate bombing campaign in Yemen that has caused many civilian casualties.
- Vietnam is a former adversary that seeks much closer security ties with the United States.
- Russia is locked in deep diplomatic conflict with the United States over Ukraine, but the two nations have worked closely to limit Iran's nuclear program, to move U.S. equipment to and from Afghanistan, and to find a solution to the Syrian civil war.

- Iran is a potential adversary of the United States, with three and a half decades of bitter history, yet Tehran is working in parallel with Washington to defeat ISIS.
- China confronts U.S. allies in the South and East China seas, but U.S.-China bilateral economic ties are vital to both countries.
- Cuba has been a U.S. adversary for over half a century, but the two nations cooperated on the Ebola crisis and recently reopened diplomatic relations.

In addition, the dynamics of key regions of the world differ markedly. Europe is pursuing with difficulty a 21st-century agenda of continental political and economic integration. East Asia is mired in a 19th-century balance of power struggle. The Middle East is contending with sectarian strife reminiscent of the 17th-century Thirty Years' War, which destroyed much of northern Europe. Given these trends, contradictions, and dynamics, flexibility and pragmatism—rather than ideological rigidity—are needed if the United States is to take full advantage of the opportunities provided by these partners and even these potential adversaries.

Alternative U.S. Approaches to Partnership Engagement

While strategy should determine resource allocation for national security, this approach may not always be feasible. A look at alternative approaches must mix ends with ways and means. Three broad potential approaches are summarized in Table 2.1.[4] They will be analyzed in subsequent chapters.

The first approach might be called assertiveness. Under this approach, the United States would lead a vigorous global effort to advance not just its interests but its values. As an exceptional nation,

---

[4] These approaches are roughly comparable to those presented in James Dobbins, Richard H. Solomon, Michael S. Chase, Ryan Henry, F. Stephen Larrabee, Robert J. Lempert, Andrew Liepman, Jeffrey Martini, David Ochmanek, and Howard J. Shatz, *Choices for America in a Turbulent World*, Santa Monica, Calif.: RAND Corporation, RR-1114-RC, 2015, p. 5.

Table 2.1
Summary of Three Alternative U.S. Approaches

	Assertiveness	Collaborative Engagement	Retrenchment
Theory	American exceptionalism	Forward partnering	Offshore balancing
Driver	Primarily values	Primarily interests	Narrow interests
Leadership	U.S. lead dominant	Joint leadership	Partners lead more
Example	Iraq 2003	Desert Storm/ISAF	Persian Gulf 1978–1990
Partners	Partners less important	Regional partnerships	Regional surrogates
Adversaries	Confront adversaries	Split adversaries	Compromise with adversaries
Use of force	Alone or small coalition	Primarily with partners	Limited use of force
Force structure	Ground forces key	Enablers for allies	Surgical/naval/air
Defense budget[a]	$650 billion–$750 billion	$500 billion–$650 billion	$400 billion–$500 billion
Major advantage	Freedom of action	Maximize partnerships	Low cost
Major problem	Limited use of partners	Partners unwilling?	U.S. disengagement creates panic
Major task	Increase defense spending	Build partner capacity	Identify surrogates

[a] These budget figures are illustrative but are based on historical analogies. The budget range for assertiveness is based on 2005–2010 defense budgets. The range for a collaborative approach is based roughly on the George H. W. Bush years. The range for retrenchment is based roughly on the Jimmy Carter years.

the United States would bear the primary burden of protecting allies and partners and pursuing American values internationally. The United States would challenge potential adversaries vigorously and not compromise much on principle. This approach is based on the neoconservative—or assertive interventionist—school. The United States would focus on finding a few capable and willing partners so that it does not have to act alone, but it would take unilateral military action if necessary. Its visionary and interventionist quality would require significantly higher defense budgets and higher numbers of ground forces than currently planned. The wars in Iraq and Afghanistan have made this approach politically unpopular.[5]

A second strategy might be called collaborative engagement.[6] If assertiveness means unapologetic leadership and championing values, collaborative engagement is characterized by joint leadership with partners and by concentrating on broad common interests, such as maintaining international rule of law. The United States would broadly maintain its current force structure but would rely increasingly on empowered partners to augment alliance postures. This has also been described as "forward partnering."[7] It emphasizes the importance of U.S. partners in meeting the multiple challenges presented by adversaries. It stresses alliance cohesion and building partner capacity. It implies much greater pressure on partners to carry their weight. The approach recognizes the limits of U.S. power, but would seek to compensate for these limits by drawing more on the capabilities of U.S. partners. It also would attempt to find greater common ground with a few potential adversaries to reduce risk. It would require considerable U.S. persuasion to stimulate partner capabilities, higher degrees

---

5 For a discussion of U.S. assertiveness in Iraq, see David C. Gompert, Hans Binnendijk, and Bonny Lin, *Blinders, Blunders and Wars: What America and China Can Learn*, Santa Monica, Calif: RAND Corporation, RR-768-RC, 2014, pp. 161–174.

6 This should not imply that the United States has been holding its partners back—it has not. Instead, it suggests the need for a much more concentrated U.S. effort to prod partners to contribute more.

7 The concept of forward partnering was first introduced by Hans Binnendijk and Frank Hoffman in a 2012 keynote address to a National Defense University conference on U.S. strategy.

of U.S. military assistance to vulnerable partners, and a willingness to develop positions in closer consultation with key partners and, at the same time, dissuade them from confrontational behavior.

A third approach might be called retrenchment.[8] It would focus U.S. national security attention on narrowly defined vital interests and pull attention away from some regions where interests are less than vital. This strategy goes beyond restraint to a more fundamental reevaluation of U.S. interests. For example, the United States might concentrate on military threats to treaty allies in Europe and Asia while reducing commitments in the Middle East. Compared with the other approaches, this strategy would also seek greater accommodation with potential adversaries to reduce the risk of conflict. U.S. force posture, at least in the Middle East, might reflect what has been called "offshore balancing." This is a somewhat more isolationist perspective that draws on the academic work of several foreign policy realists who believe that the United States is overextended and that engagement should concentrate on narrow U.S. interests rather than values.[9] Offshore balancing would have the United States choose a few key regional surrogates to champion common policies in its region. It would require a smaller defense budget than the other two alternatives.

These three approaches represent specific points on a broader spectrum of national security policies and, as such, are illustrative. Each approach could be disassembled and reassembled using different

---

8 For a recent example of the case for retrenchment, see David A. Shlapak "Towards a More Modest American Strategy," *Survival: Global Politics and Strategy*, Vol. 57, No. 2, 2015, pp. 59–78. For additional examples, see Christopher A. Preble, *The Power Problem*, Ithaca, N.Y.: Cornell University Press, 2009; Walter A. McDougall, *Promised Land, Crusader State: The American Encounter with the World Since 1776*, Boston, Mass.: Houghton Mifflin, 1997; Stephen M. Walt, *Taming America's Power: The Global Response to U.S. Primacy*, New York: W. W. Norton and Company, 2005; Christopher Layne, *The Peace of Illusions: American Grand Strategy from 1940 to the Present*, Ithaca, N.Y.: Cornell University Press, 2006; Barry R. Posen, *Restraint: A New Foundation for U.S. Grand Strategy*, Ithaca, N.Y.: Cornell University Press, 2014; and John J. Mearsheimer, "Imperial By Design," *The National Interest*, No. 111, January/February 2011.

9 Academic proponents of offshore balancing include John J. Mearsheimer, Stephen M. Walt, Christopher Layne, and others.

criteria. However, they are used here for analytical purposes because each has some historical antecedents. For example:

- The George W. Bush administration pursued an assertive national security policy, which included the notion of preemption and a strong willingness to act alone when necessary. It was primarily a values-based policy designed to promote regime change to eliminate threats and develop democratic nations. Partners were at one point described as being either "for us or against us." Defense budgets rose to well over $700 billion annually.
- The George H. W. Bush administration took a more collaborative, pragmatic, and interests-based approach. It coordinated carefully with allies and adversaries to manage the end of the Cold War and assembled a large international coalition for Operation Desert Storm. The so-called Powell Doctrine, with its emphasis on vital national interests and circumspect use of force, tended to guide its thinking.[10] The 1990 defense budget was about $525 billion (in 2011 dollars).[11]
- The Carter administration followed a policy of retrenchment after the end of the Vietnam War, modified somewhat after the Soviet invasion of Afghanistan. Carter stressed human rights, arms sales restraint, and limited military intervention. The Carter defense budget averaged about $375 billion (in 2011 dollars).

---

[10] General Colin Powell suggested that the following questions should be answered before the United States committed troops to war:

- Is a vital national security interest threatened?
- Do we have a clear, attainable objective?
- Have the risks and costs been fully and frankly analyzed?
- Have all other non-violent policy means been fully exhausted?
- Is there a plausible exit strategy to avoid endless entanglement?
- Have the consequences of our actions been fully considered?
- Is the action supported by the American people?
- Do we have genuine, broad international support?

[11] Stockholm International Peace Research Institute, "SIPRI Military Expenditure Database," spreadsheet data, undated.

The Obama administration's base defense budget has hovered around $525 billion in current dollars, with increases for overseas contingency operations. The administration's approach is close to collaboration, but includes elements of restraint. The 2015 *National Security Strategy* suggests the need to lead with capable allies, prioritize, resist overreach, and maintain strategic patience and persistence.[12] That document makes 94 references to partners and allies. Similarly, the 2015 *National Military Strategy* calls U.S. partners a "unique strength."[13]

---

[12] The White House, *National Security Strategy*, Washington, D.C., February 2015.

[13] Joint Chiefs of Staff, *The National Military Strategy of the United States of America*, Washington, D.C., 2015, p. 9.

CHAPTER THREE

Anatomy of the Potential Adversaries

This chapter will review the general nature of the challenge to U.S. interests and the liberal democratic order posed by the United States' most serious potential adversaries. As the 2015 *National Military Strategy* states, "Today and into the foreseeable future, we must pay greater attention to challenges posed by state actors."[1] In each case, the threat that state actors pose to the United States or its allies is on the rise. The chart in Figure 3.1 catalogues these adversaries in terms of both the nature of their differences with the United States (from irreconcilable differences to sharing some common interests; see Table 3.1) and the nature of the military, economic, and political threat that they might pose (from limited to full spectrum). Separating them in this way can improve our ability to understand their nature and to manage them in a global context. They are discussed in order of their global power.

China

The National Intelligence Council's *Global Trends 2030* report projects that China will surpass all of Europe in terms of its "global power index" in the next few decades and that it will surpass the United States in the next 30 years (given straight-line projections).[2] Between

---

1 Joint Chiefs of Staff, 2015, p. 3.

2 U.S. National Intelligence Council, 2012, pp. 16–17. Some of the material in this section is drawn from a RAND working group meeting organized by Eric Heginbotham. It includes suggestions made by Richard Solomon.

Figure 3.1
Potential U.S. Adversaries

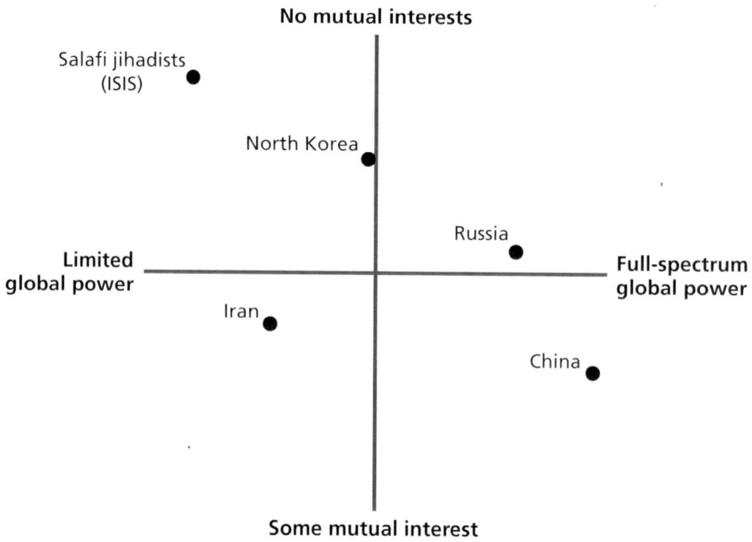

NOTES: Based roughly on defense spending, GDP, population, and nuclear capability. The positioning of each state is illustrative.

ISIS has very limited resources, population, and technical capacity. It is nonetheless dangerous, with its ruthlessness and potential international reach through terrorist activity.

Iran has an annual GDP of about $370 billion, a population of about 80 million, a defense budget of $10 billion–$15 billion, and an active covert military capability.

North Korea has only 25 million people and an annual GDP of about $40 billion. Its defense budget is estimated at about $10 billion. It is particularly dangerous because it has an active-duty military force of about 1.2 million, artillery that threatens Seoul, nuclear weapons, and a budding intercontinental ballistic missile (ICBM) program that could soon threaten the United States.

Russia has an annual GDP of about $2.1 trillion, a population of 145 million, a defense budget of about $81 billion in 2015, and parity with the United States in strategic nuclear weapons. It could have short-term strategic advantage in conventional military operations near its border.

China's annual GDP is approaching $10 trillion, its defense budget may now exceed $200 billion, it has the world's largest population, and it possesses a significant number of nuclear warheads. Its anti-access/area-denial capabilities are well developed.

RAND *RR1210-3.1*

Table 3.1
U.S. Common Interest with Potential Adversaries

	Values	Strategic Interests	Economic Interests
China	Low	Medium	High
Russia	Low	Low	Medium
Iran	Low	Medium	Medium
North Korea	Zero	Low	Zero
ISIS	Zero	Zero	Zero

2015 and 2030, China will become the world's largest consumer of oil, coal, and steel. Its aggressive global resource-extraction policy reflects this growing need. In that time frame, between 44 percent and 55 percent of all new global shipbuilding will be Chinese.[3] Its reliance on trade and ocean transit will only increase.

Estimates of China's growing power mask its vulnerability. Economic growth is highly uneven and corruption is rampant. Pollution and environmental damage make daily life dangerous. Reliance on trade creates dependencies. Its stock market has proven to be volatile. The Chinese government professes a communist ideology but practices a form of state capitalism. Many liken the Chinese economy to a bicycle that requires continuous forward motion to remain erect. President Xi Jinping has quickly consolidated power through his anticorruption campaign to gain control over this vulnerable situation. He may have little margin for error.

Beijing's sense of emerging power translates into a desire to be able to modify the rules of the international system if those rules conflict with Chinese interests.[4] The country's leadership sees China as a historical victim, having suffered "a hundred years of humiliation," and feels that China has earned the right to a new seat at the table. This attitude

---

[3] QinetiQ, Lloyd's Register, and the University of Strathclyde Glasgow, 2013, pp. 83, 90. Also, see Binnendijk, 2014a, pp. 9–13, for more details on growing Chinese strength.

[4] See Nina Hachigian, ed., *Debating China: The U.S.-China Relationship in Ten Conversations*, Oxford: Oxford University Press, 2014.

creates new tensions in the region. For example, China argues that its domestic laws override international laws relating to territorial seas and aircraft overflight rights. It is unwilling to implement the ASEAN (Association of Southeast Asian Nations) Code of Conduct for dispute settlement. At the same time, the Chinese leadership believes that the United States has maneuvered against Chinese interests in institutions such as the International Monetary Fund (IMF) and that Washington excludes Beijing from trade talks.

As a result, China is seeking to create parallel systems.[5] For example, China established the Shanghai Cooperation Organization in 1996, which was designed for Eurasian political, economic, and security cooperation.[6] Xi has spoken about creating a new Asia-Pacific security architecture, which may or may not include the United States. Additionally, China has sought to create a "new type of great power relations" tie with the United States that, in China's view, would be modeled on two decades of Sino-Russian relations. That construct would acknowledge great power spheres of influence, defer to United Nations authority where China has a veto, accommodate great power core interests, downplay collective security arrangements, and subjugate customary international law to the interests of great powers. It might be described as a return to a 19th-century concept of national power.[7]

In the economic arena, China has proposed creation of an Asian free trade zone and a new Asian Infrastructure Investment Bank (AIIB), which now has 46 founding members, including some of the United States' closest Asian and European partners. This is related to China's new "one belt, one road" policy, designed to link countries along the historic Silk Road trade route and countries in Southeast Asia and South Asia to China in a web of new energy and transport

---

5 Hachigian, 2014.

6 The Shanghai Cooperation Organization has six members (China, Russia, Kazakhstan, Kyrgyzstan, Tajikistan, and Uzbekistan), five observers (Afghanistan, India, Iran, Mongolia, and Pakistan), and three dialogue partners (Belarus, Sri Lanka, and Turkey).

7 Paul Mancinelli, "Conceptualizing 'New Type Great Power Relations': The Sino-Russian Model," *China Brief*, Vol. 14, No. 9, 2014.

infrastructure projects, cultural exchanges, and trade. These are China's answers to U.S. and Japanese efforts to limit its voting power in the IMF and Asian Development Bank, as well as the U.S.-led Trans Pacific Partnership negotiations, which now exclude China. The AIIB focuses on infrastructure development as the key to sustained economic growth. These proposals are accompanied by promises of trillions of dollars of future trade with China's neighbors. China has also created the China-ASEAN Investment Cooperation Fund, sponsored by its Export-Import Bank. Asian countries are attracted to the prospects of Chinese-led growth.

China's growing nationalism, its need to protect sea lanes, and its sense of entitlement and encirclement is reflected in its dramatic defense buildup. The U.S. Defense Department estimates that China's defense budget for 2012 was between $135 billion and $215 billion, with an annual growth rate of nearly 10 percent over the past decade.[8] China's 2013 Defense White Paper called for armed forces "commensurate with China's international standing."[9] Some estimate that, by 2030, China's defense budget could match that of the United States. The People's Liberation Army (PLA) is transforming its conventional forces using modern information technology. The PLA considers the United States to be its primary adversary and exercises accordingly. This combination will create a formidable obstacle for the possible use of U.S. military power in the region. Within ten years, China may possess an anti-access and area denial (A2/AD) capability that could significantly limit the degree to which the U.S. Navy and Air Force can operate within the first island chain. China seeks "places, not bases" for its navy to better protect trade routes and commercial interests. In addition, China currently has a full spectrum of military power that includes a significant number of nuclear weapons, 50–75 ICBMs (including the long-range DF-31A),[10] space assets, and capable cyber

[8] Office of the Secretary of Defense, *Annual Report to the Congress on Military and Security Developments Involving the People's Republic of China*, Washington, D.C., 2013, p. 45.

[9] International Institute for Strategic Studies (IISS), *The Military Balance 2014*, London, February 5, 2014, p. 206.

[10] Nuclear Threat Initiative, "Country Profiles: China," web page, updated July 2015.

operations. In that sense, China could pose an existential threat to the United States.

In previous decades, China has fought border wars with Russia, India, and Vietnam over territorial disputes. The results were generally disadvantageous for China, but Beijing's primary strategic purpose today seems to have turned from those land-based disputes to advancing its maritime claims. Its 2015 Defense White Paper stresses its expanding national security interests and shifts emphasis to both naval power and cyber operations.[11]

In 2009, the United Nations Law of the Seas Commission on Limits of the Continental Shelf set a deadline to record those contending claims. Vietnam, the Philippines, Malaysia, and others separately and jointly submitted their claims. China protested and filed its own extensive claims of "indisputable sovereignty" over most of the South China Sea, based on historical discovery.[12] China claims a "nine-dash line" in the South China Sea that has little historical basis and encompasses some 90 percent of the entire sea—to the exclusion of all of its neighbors. That area contains the Paracel Islands (occupied by China but claimed by Vietnam), the Spratly Islands (disputed by China, the Philippines, Brunei, Malaysia, Taiwan, and Vietnam, with various nations occupying specific islands), and the Scarborough Shoal (also claimed by the Philippines). Strategic control over heavily trafficked sea lanes, as well as oil and fishing rights, is at stake. China is willing to negotiate with its neighbors bilaterally on the contending claims where China would have considerable leverage, while China's neighbors want multilateral talks.

Perhaps most dangerous—from the U.S. perspective—is China's extension of its claim to the Senkaku (Diaoyu) Islands, long administered by Japan, and its establishment of an Air Defense Identification Zone that overlaps the Japanese zone. The Japanese government's

---

[11] Dennis J. Blasko, "The 2015 Chinese Defense White Paper on Strategy in Perspective: Maritime Missions Require a Change in the PLA Mindset," *China Brief*, Vol. 15, No. 12, May 29, 2015.

[12] Carlyle A. Thayer, "South China Sea: A Commons for China Only?" *Yale Global* online, July 7, 2011.

attempt to purchase several of the islands from a private Japanese owner raised the stakes for China. The U.S. defense commitment to Japan has been extended to those islands. The United States has no treaty commitments to defend islands in the South China Sea; its interests there rest on freedom of navigation and overflight.

Some believe China now wishes to turn the South and East China seas into Chinese lakes. In fairness, China's neighbors also have contending claims and China does not want to lose the competition by being meek. But China's maritime claims are extreme; it strengthens those claims with oil exploration, fishing fleets, military operations, and construction of new islands and military bases, such as the planned airstrip and sea-berth at an artificial island called Fiery Cross Reef.[13] China also challenges U.S. intelligence flights in international waters and is building defense capabilities to threaten navies operating in its "lake." This constitutes a potentially serious challenge to freedom of the seas and heightens the threat of confrontation with its neighbors.[14]

The United States is taking additional steps to monitor events in these contested regions, thereby enhancing transparency. It does not take a position on specific claims but seeks peaceful resolution of the contending claims and reiterates its firm position on freedom of navigation. To reinforce its right to free movement in international air space, the United States continues to fly intelligence missions near the Chinese coast, but well outside China's 12-mile sovereign territory. The United States has also recently flown two B-52s near the newly constructed islands. Chinese fighter aircraft harass these missions at high speeds.[15] Escalation of an incident, particularly in the East China Sea, could drag the United States into conflict with China.

---

[13] For further analysis, see Julian Lindley-French, "China's Fiery Cross?" Lindley-French's Blog Blast: Speaking Truth unto Power, blog post, September 9, 2014.

[14] The United States would have better standing to challenge Chinese claims if it ratified the United Nations Convention on the Law of the Sea.

[15] Such maneuvers caused the April 2001 Hainan Island incident, in which a Chinese fighter jet collided with a U.S. Navy EP-3 intelligence aircraft, leading to an international dispute between the two countries.

The maritime claims have backfired on China's efforts to gain political influence in Asia. A 2014 Pew Research Center poll indicated that in "all 11 Asian nations polled, roughly half or more say they are concerned that territorial disputes between China and its neighbors will lead to a military conflict. This includes a remarkably high 93% of Filipinos, 85% of Japanese, 84% of Vietnamese, and 83% of South Koreans."[16] Throughout the area, U.S. allies and partners—as well as one former enemy, Vietnam—are seeking ways to strengthen their ties to the United States. The Chinese leadership tends to believe that the United States has orchestrated these complaints, which fuels its concern about being contained.

China and the United States differ on an array of other issues, often relating to values. The United States sees human rights as universal and applying to individuals, while Chinese leaders fear a return to the chaos of the Cultural Revolution and prize stability and collective rights over individual rights.[17] The Chinese engage in 21st-century cyber espionage on a global scale. (They are not alone.) Chinese trade practices are mercantile.

And yet there are considerable areas in which Chinese and American interests overlap. China and the United States could both face catastrophic consequences should events drive them into conflict, which, once begun, would be quite difficult to terminate. The two nations are highly dependent on each other economically. Their annual bilateral trade is estimated at more than half a trillion dollars.[18] About one-third of China's $4 trillion in foreign reserves is held in U.S. dollars, making the two nations mutually dependent. The Chinese leadership has lifted 500 million of its people out of poverty since it began market reforms in 1978 and continues to prioritize increasing income and building national economic power.

---

[16] Pew Research Center, "Global Opposition to U.S. Surveillance and Drones, but Limited Harm to America's Image: Many in Asia Worry About Conflict with China," web page, July 14, 2014.

[17] Of the ten most deadly human conflicts in recorded history, five involve Chinese civil wars.

[18] Binnendijk, 2014a, p. 274.

Areas of possible common interest were the topic of a high-level meeting during the June 2015 U.S.-China Strategic and Economic Dialogue. Most of the 127 items contained in the strategic dialogue summary alone covered areas of some overlapping interest. These items call for greater "positive military to military interaction" and included military early warning and communications, notifications of major military actions, rules of behavior for safety of air and sea encounters, nuclear safety, shale gas and oil exploration, non-proliferation, counter-narcotics, law enforcement, counterterrorism, anti-corruption, customs cooperation, space cooperation, container security, consular exchanges, and maritime security.[19]

In November 2014, two developments moved U.S.-Chinese relations in a more positive direction. First, Chinese and Japanese representatives reached a "Shanghai Communiqué–like" agreement on the Senkaku Islands issue, under which both sides recognized that there is a dispute over the waters surrounding the islands. This gives China international recognition that a dispute exists, but since the reference was to "waters around" the islands, Japan does not need to backtrack on the issue of sovereignty of the islands themselves. It is unclear whether this diplomatic nicety will defuse this dangerous issue. Second, during the Asia-Pacific Economic Cooperation Summit, the United States and China agreed to cap greenhouse gases by 2030 and to remove tariffs on $1 trillion of annual trade in information and communications technology.[20]

President Xi Jinping's September 2015 state visit to Washington aimed to further enhance the prospect of bilateral cooperation, including a series of agreements on cybersecurity and cybercrime, military cooperation on air-to-air safety and crisis communications, strengthening cooperation on development assistance, nuclear security, and counterterrorism.

---

[19] U.S. Department of State, "U.S.-China Strategic and Economic Dialogue Outcomes of the Strategic Track," media note, Washington, D.C., June 24, 2015.

[20] David Nakamura and Steven Mufson, "U.S. and China Announce Climate Deal," *Washington Post*, November 12, 2014.

China will certainly be the principal strategic competitor of the United States in the decades to come, yet the two rivals share significant overlapping interests. The challenge for the United States is to manage this complex relationship with China, with an understanding of the strategic possibilities, but without compromising its alliances and freedom of the seas. A higher degree of direct engagement with China would be in the U.S. interest. Chapter Seven includes suggestions for managing the United States' relationship with China.

Russia

After China, Russia is the United States' most formidable potential foe.[21] Russia has parity in strategic nuclear weapons, superiority in non-strategic nuclear weapons, and, despite a conventional imbalance with NATO, has definite local military advantages in several "gray areas" between itself and NATO and even in the Baltic states. Russian defense spending has roughly tripled since 2000 and currently ranks third in the world, at over $80 billion per year. The weak Russian conventional forces of two decades ago have been modernized and are well trained. The 2015 Victory in Europe Day (V-E Day) military parade in Moscow's Red Square was the largest in history, making a political point. Recent snap exercises and a rapid deployment to Syria demonstrate Russia's ability to mobilize and willingness to use force.

Although Russia has been considered to be a U.S. strategic partner for the past two decades, Moscow's recent aggression in Ukraine and elsewhere has put Russia on an increasingly hostile path that may be difficult to reverse. The combination of advanced capabilities and limited common interests could make Russia one of the most dangerous adversaries for the United States and its NATO allies. The shift from partnership to potential foe developed slowly, as President Vladimir Putin stoked grievances against the West for NATO enlargement, abrogation of the Anti–Ballistic Missile Treaty, use of force without United Nations (UN) Security Council approval, and interference in

---

[21] This section includes input by Andrew Weiss.

Russia's internal affairs. A key marker in this process was Putin's 2007 speech at the Munich Security Conference, wherein he surprised the audience by lashing out at Western policies.

While China is clearly an ascending power, Russia's prospects are harder to discern. To many in the West, Russia appears to be in decline, with serious demographic and economic problems. Its fundamental strengths are hydrocarbon exports, nuclear weapons, and a growing conventional defense capability, but energy exports may be a wasting asset and nuclear weapons can be used only for intimidation or ultimate self-defense. This negative portrait is disputed by many Russian policymakers, who feel that Russia has restored its great-power status and will no longer bend before external actors such as the United States.

Putin has created his own model of government to confront Western liberal democracy. This model consists of a macho persona, attacks on Western morality, authoritarian control at home, defense buildup, an avowed responsibility to protect Russian speakers everywhere, the use of various types of coercion and blackmail against his enemies in Russia and abroad, a "turn to the East," and efforts to exert Russian political and economic dominance through a so-called Eurasian Economic Union. His message is reinforced daily by the government-dominated media and even in new school textbooks designed to stimulate Russian nationalism. This model has attracted right-wing sympathy in parts of Europe, including Marine Le Pen's National Front and the Hungarian government of Victor Orban. While Putin's efforts cannot reverse the damaging effects of international sanctions imposed after his annexation of Crimea and incursions into Ukraine, his strategy appears to be to keep Western partners off-balance and strengthen his own political position.

When initially peaceful demonstrations in Ukraine ousted President Victor Yanukovych in 2014, a series of events have occurred that threaten to re-polarize Europe. Under pressure from Putin, Yanukovych rejected an offer for an Association Agreement with the European Union (EU) and was subsequently forced to flee Kiev by pro-EU demonstrations. Nationalists in the Ukrainian Parliament tried but failed to repeal legislation making Russian a second official language.

The Russian Parliament, in turn, authorized the invasion of Ukraine to protect the Russian minority. Moscow saw the ouster of Yanukovych as a Western-inspired coup against a Russian-backed government, while in the West it was seen as a peaceful uprising against a corrupt government. Putin seized Crimea and held an unrecognized referendum to justify annexation. Russia then encouraged separatist militias in the Donbas area of Ukraine with personnel, weapons, and intelligence. After an initial attempt to stop the fighting failed with the first Minsk Protocol, a second—Minsk II—ceasefire agreement was brokered by Germany and France in February 2015. Despite local violations, it remains unclear whether Russia will abide by this agreement or eventually seek a land bridge from its border to Crimea.

Putin has used an array of tools to agitate, intimidate, and coerce while trying to limit the Western response and avoid crossing too many Western red lines. Referred to in the West as hybrid or asymmetric warfare, Russia's strategy has included cyber operations, blatantly false and alarming propaganda, snap military exercises near neighbors' borders, energy cutoffs, paramilitary operations, issuance of Russian passports in Crimea, agitation among Russian speakers, signature drives calling for independence for Russian-speaking areas, humanitarian truck convoys, outright military intervention, and political annexation.

One of the most threatening of Russia's stances is its repeated references to the possibility of limited nuclear attacks on Baltic, Polish, and even Danish cities. These threats include Russian military exercises ending in feigned nuclear strikes and comments by far-right commentators unchallenged by the Kremlin.[22] One of the most dangerous of Putin's maneuvers is his effort to send Russian aircraft and submarines on patrols near or into the sovereign territory of his neighbors. In 2014, NATO intercepted more than 100 Russian aircraft, and the frequency of these intercepts is increasing.[23] Concern over potential esca-

[22] Several Russian military exercises have ended with simulated nuclear attacks on Warsaw, while outlandish statements by Vladimir Zhirinovsky and others are allowed to stand without Kremlin rebuttal. See Anne Applebaum, "Is It 1939 Again in Europe?" *Washington Post*, August 31, 2014.

[23] Michael Birnbaum, "NATO Intercepts Several Russian Jets," *Washington Post*, October 30, 2014b.

lation was highlighted recently by Graham Allison and Dimitri Simes. They argued that domestic Russian politics and a Ukraine crisis could trigger a "sleepwalking" reaction similar to the dynamics that caused World War I.[24]

Putin's provocations have not been limited to Europe. In August 2014, Russia conducted military exercises in the southern Kuril Islands (or Northern Territories), which Japan considered an affront. The Japanese saw the exercises as violating the April 2013 Putin-Abe agreement to seek a peaceful solution to their contending claims.[25] In the Arctic, Russia has made extravagant maritime claims and is building naval and air facilities to defend those claims.[26] In Syria, Russia has deployed advanced Sukhoi-34 fighters that are attacking both Islamic State and Free Syrian Army targets.

Putin's stated goal is to protect the rights of Russian speakers in neighboring countries. His broader goal is to regain as much Russian power as he can without starting a conflict with NATO or suffering crippling sanctions. He has pursued that goal with effective propaganda, stirring deep Russian nationalism. His popularity in opinion polls has risen above 85 percent. He has accumulated a series of short-term victories, but the long-term consequences for the Russian economy and Russian ties to the West could be crippling.

The risk is that Putin will continue to overreach. History shows that when bold leaders are filled with hubris, they underestimate their adversaries and can blunder badly.[27] This concern has led NATO planners to begin considering a nightmare scenario in which Russia launches a conventional attack on one or more of the Baltic states and threatens nuclear retaliation should NATO seek to regain occupied ter-

---

[24] Graham Allison and Dimitri Simes, "Stumbling into War," *The National Interest*, May/June 2015.

[25] Zachary Keck, "Russia Conducts Military Drill on Disputed Kuril Islands," *The Diplomat*, August 13, 2014.

[26] See Vladimir Isachenkov, "Russia Submits Revised Claim for Vast Arctic Seabed Territories at United Nations," *Associated Press*, August 4, 2015.

[27] David Gompert and Hans Binnendijk, "Will Putin Fall Victim to One of History's Classic Blunders?" *The RAND Blog*, April 14, 2014a.

ritory. While that scenario is inconsistent with Putin's current policy of cautious aggression, Putin's rhetoric lends it some credence. As NATO takes steps to deter both hybrid threats and this nightmare scenario, there is increased risk that military exercises on both sides will create incidents that could escalate. Weak political communications at the most-senior levels of government might make it difficult to control such escalation.

While Putin's course seems difficult to reverse, a set of overlapping interests with the West still exists. Russia is betting that, over time, sanctions placed on Russia's economy will also impose costs on the West, particularly in Europe, and that the sanctions regime will collapse. Despite his bluster, Putin probably wants to avoid direct military confrontation with the West. In May 2015 talks with German Chancellor Angela Merkel, he tried to seek some more common ground with the West. With Russia's sovereign wealth funds shrinking, Putin may wish to avoid a costly arms race, which he is certain to lose. His efforts to develop partnerships elsewhere have had limited success. The United States and Russia continue to share some common interests in managing nuclear weapons, terrorism, piracy, narcotics, the environment, Iran, Afghanistan, the Arctic, and North Korea. In the P5+1 (China, France, Russia, United Kingdom, United States, and Germany) negotiations over the future of Iran's nuclear program, Russia has been constructive, but it also sold S-300 air defense missiles to Iran. The United States and Russia cooperated to remove chemical weapons from Syria; further cooperation will be necessary to end Syria's civil war. Each common interest should be explored. NATO's efforts to strengthen its common defense commitment and halt its defense-spending slide will be noticed in Moscow, but those efforts are unlikely to serve as an incentive for Moscow to reverse the downward slide in relations. The image of a "Fortress Russia" besieged by Western enemies appears to be increasingly useful to Putin.

Russian Foreign Minister Sergey Lavrov has called for a Reset 2.0, but a U.S.-Russia strategic partnership is not feasible in the wake of the annexation of Crimea. Nonetheless, Putin needs to be given off-ramps to begin to reverse his current behavior. Much will depend on how the Ukraine crisis is resolved. If the Minsk II ceasefire is implemented, Western economic sanctions on Russia might be gradually lifted and a new equilibrium could be created. Finding that new equilibrium with Putin's Moscow somewhere between strategic partnership and another Cold War would be the task of American policymakers. Identifying institutions and procedures to manage that new relationship will be important.

North Korea

The Democratic People's Republic of Korea (DPRK) ranks third among potential adversaries in terms of its capability to directly harm the United States. It ranks near last in common interests. While China, Russia, and Iran are potential military adversaries for the United States, each has at least some overlapping interests with the United States that might serve as a basis for some eventual improvement of the relationships. The "hermit kingdom" shares no values or economic interests with the United States. *Juche*, DPRK's political philosophy of self-reliance, is more of a religion that deifies the Kim family and sets their philosophy above international law.[28] It has no application elsewhere and hence serves as no model for others.

This clash of values leaves little room for mutual understanding or engagement. Under *Juche*, North Korea has built massive concentration camps for political prisoners and suffered famine, at the cost of millions of lives.[29] Belligerence is the DPRK's only negotiating tool and it wields it constantly. The sole opportunity for continued engagement is the Six-Party Talks on denuclearizing North Korea, but that negotiation has been stalled for six years.

The unpredictability of North Korean behavior, such as the 2010 sinking of the *Cheonan* or the artillery attack on Yeonpyeong Island, combined with South Korea's increasing unwillingness to tolerate such

---

[28] See Grace Lee, "The Political Philosophy of Juche," *Stanford Journal of East Asian Affairs*, Vol. 3, No. 1, Spring 2003, p. 105.

[29] Currently there are four camps with 80,000 to 120,000 inmates. See "North Korea's Crimes Against Humanity Have 'No Parallel' Today," *Washington Post*, February 19, 2014.

actions, has put militaries on the peninsula on a hair trigger. The United States has 28,500 troops deployed in the Republic of Korea (ROK, or South Korea) and a firm treaty commitment to defend that nation. The United States retains command of all ROK and U.S. forces under the UN Combined Forces Command structure, an arrangement that the United States has sought to change but the ROK prefers because of the setup's deterrent effect. Given the consequences of a mistake on the peninsula, maintaining U.S. control for a while longer may be wise.

The United States seems to have run out of options in dealing with North Korea. It has faced off against North Korean troops since the armistice of 1953. Hopes that the young leader Kim Jong Un might learn from his experience in Switzerland and bring reform to Pyongyang were soon dashed. He demonstrated his ruthlessness by executing his uncle and many others in the top leadership. Instead of instituting economic reforms on the Chinese model, he emphasized North Korea's nuclear weapons and missile development program. He has purged several older general officers, replaced them with younger officers more likely to be loyal to him, and shifted power back to the Communist Party.[30]

DPRK engineers are making progress on the accuracy and range of DPRK missile systems.[31] Assessments are mixed, with some analysts suggesting that DPRK ballistic missile reliability is low but that progress is being made on warhead miniaturization.[32] In June 2014, Admiral William Gortney, of the North American Aerospace Defense Command, assessed that the long-range KN-08 is "operational today."[33] Those devices could be delivered in other ways (e.g., by suicide submarines). U.S. allies South Korea and Japan are in range of DPRK

[30] IISS, 2014, p. 217.

[31] David E. Sanger, "U.S. Confronts Consequences of Underestimating North Korean Leader," *Washington Post,* April 25, 2014.

[32] See "North Korea Able to Miniaturize Nukes: DOD Intel Arm," *NTI Global Security Newswire,* April 12, 2013, and Dan Lamothe, "U.S. General: North Korea Likely Can Build Miniaturized Nuclear Weapons," *Washington Post,* October 24, 2014.

[33] Daniel Wasserbly, "U.S. Military Views North Korea's ICBM as Operational," *IHS Jane's 360,* April 8, 2015.

missiles, and the United States might soon be if the TPD-2 is further refined.[34] Major efforts have been made by Pyongyang to prevent a preemptive attack by hardening missile storage areas and making those missiles mobile.

On the conventional front, the million-man DPRK military is not well trained or equipped, but its size, proximity to Seoul, special forces, 8,000 artillery, plus 5,000 rocket launchers place the ROK at great risk. Any attack could include some nuclear event.[35]

China is still the key to dealing with North Korea. The DPRK is heavily dependent on Beijing for food and other resources. China is willing to put some pressure on Pyongyang on nuclear issues, but there are limits. China would not want to see Korea united under a pro-U.S. regime. It is unwilling to discuss DPRK collapse scenarios, which could prove quite dangerous, for fear that such discussions might contribute to instability.[36] But cooperation between China and North Korea may also be more fragile than previously thought. Beijing's concerns have been growing since Pyongyang's first nuclear test and are exacerbated by Kim Jong Un's behavior. Some analysts now believe that China may no longer be as opposed to Korean unification as before.[37]

With little room to maneuver diplomatically or militarily, the Obama administration has put the North Korean problem on a back-burner. However, the problem may only get worse as the DPRK's technology improves. The United States must retain its deterrent posture and seek ways to preempt if absolutely necessary. It needs to constrain Seoul should another North-South clash take place. And, it needs to convince China to be more helpful in managing the situation.

---

[34] IISS's *Military Balance* report judges that North Korea is five years away from being able to deploy ICBMs. See IISS, 2014, p. 216.

[35] Sanger, 2014.

[36] Based on author's efforts while in government to initiate such discussions.

[37] Jonathan Pollack, "Is Xi Jinping Rethinking Korean Unification?" briefing, Brookings, January 20, 2015.

Iran

In addition to China, Iran presents a good opportunity for the United States to capitalize on some common interests with a long-time adversary and to reduce the potential for conflict with a fairly capable foe. There are two clusters of issues to consider when assessing the future relationship with Iran. The first is the nature of the July 2015 nuclear deal; the second is Iran's broader role in the Middle East.

The United States broke diplomatic relations with Iran in 1980, following the November 1979 embassy takeover and subsequent hostage crisis. More than three decades of mutual hostility ensued. Harsh treatment under Ayatollah Ruhollah Khomeini for those in opposition to the Islamic Republic left tens of thousands dead. During the Iran-Iraq War, the United States sided with Iraqi dictator Saddam Hussein. From 2009 to 2010, the United States was sympathetic to those protesting election irregularities that kept former President Mahmoud Ahmadinejad in power. But actual Western support for that failed "Green Revolution" was limited.

Nonetheless, the same moderate forces in Iran that drove the Green Revolution led to change through the ballot box. In June 2013, President Hassan Rouhani received a clear electoral mandate to seek an end to international sanctions that crippled the Iranian economy. That meant negotiating a new arrangement on Iran's nuclear program.

On April 2, 2015, negotiators in Lausanne, Switzerland, announced a framework agreement between the P5+1 and Iran. On July 14 in Vienna, a final agreement was reached that President Obama said cuts off every Iranian pathway to a nuclear weapon.[38] While a majority of the Congress opposed the Iran agreement, assurances pro-

---

[38] On November 24, 2013, Iranian Foreign Minister Javad Zarif signed a Joint Action Plan and agreed to refrain from enriching to 20-percent Uranium-235, dilute one-half of its lower-grade uranium, and provide the International Atomic Energy Agency (IAEA) greater access to Iranian facilities. Western nations agreed, in return, to refrain from imposing new sanctions and to free about $4.2 billion of previously frozen Iranian accounts. On April 2, 2015, negotiators in Lausanne reached an agreement in principle on a final deal, based in part on that interim agreement. On July 14, 2015, negotiators in Vienna reached a final detailed agreement. Based on reporting by the *New York Times* and the *Washington Post* on July 15, 2015, the final deal would include the following:

vided by President Obama in an August 19 letter to Representative Jerrold Nadler (D-NY), as well as other commitments, garnered enough Democratic support to block a resolution in the Senate disapproving the deal.[39] The strongest argument for the deal was that the other alternatives were more onerous.[40]

- Iran would cap its centrifuges at 5,060, down from some 19,000 today. All capped centrifuges would be first-generation varieties and located in one place. Iran could continue research on advanced centrifuges at the Fordow facility but cannot deploy them under the cap. This centrifuge cap would remain in effect for ten years.
- Iran would reduce its stockpile of low enriched uranium from the current 10,000 kilograms to 300 kilograms. That remaining stockpile could be enriched only up to 3.67 percent. That cap of 300 kilograms would remain in effect for 15 years.
- Iran would convert its Arak heavy-water reactor so that it would be unable to produce weapons grade plutonium.
- Iran would not have to dismantle any existing nuclear facilities.
- Verification would be "where necessary, when necessary." IAEA inspections would have access to all nuclear sites, uranium mines and mills, centrifuge plants, supply chains, and suspicious sites. If a verification issue arises, the United States and European negotiators could force an inspection; Iran, Russia, and Chins do not have a veto.
- Economic sanctions would be lifted only after the IAEA verifies that Iran has taken the agreed steps. The short-term economic advantage to Iran from the lifting of sanctions is estimated at $150 billion.
- The UN arms embargo on conventional weapons sales to Iran would be lifted after five years; the embargo on missile technology would end after eïght years; the lifting of both embargoes is subject to review procedures.
- Sanctions could "snap back" if only one of the negotiating parties declares that Iran is in substantial violation of the provisions of the agreement, though re-imposition of sanctions might prove politically difficult.

[39] Jonathan Weisman, "In Letter, Obama Tells Congress U.S. Will Still Press Iran," *Washington Post*, August 21, 2015. Also see Hans Binnendijk, "Conditions for the Iran Nuclear Deal," *Defense News*, August 16, 2015.

[40] Those alternatives included the following:

- Implementation of the deal by the United States' negotiating partners without U.S. participation. This, however, could lead to weaker implementation and distress in Europe over U.S. behavior.
- Continued economic sanctions in an effort to seek what critics would consider to be a "better" negotiated deal. This option is not very credible because those sanctions would require international cooperation, which would be difficult to maintain if the United States were to renege on the current deal. Further, Iranian negotiators

The broader question of Iran's relationship with the United States also remains uncertain. The Obama administration hopes that the nuclear agreement could change some of Iran's aggressive behavior in the region. The outcome remains uncertain. Ayatollah Khomeini has noted that the nuclear deal would not indicate a shift in Iranian thinking about its activities in the region. However, President Rouhani has countered that the agreement is the "beginning for creating an atmosphere of friendship and cooperation with various countries."[41] Iran is an authoritarian theocracy in which elections are held for political office, but religious leaders are still in ultimate control of critical decisions. Iran's influence in the region has grown in recent years, in part because Iran took advantage of the disruption created by the U.S. invasions of Iraq and Afghanistan. Iran supports Bashar al-Assad in Syria, Hezbollah in Lebanon, Hamas in Gaza, the Houthis in Yemen, and now has strong influence over Iraq's Shi'a leadership. Iran is a rival of many traditional Sunni partners of the United States, including Saudi

---

probably reached the limit of what Ayatollah Ali Khamenei and other conservative religious leaders would accept.

- Establishment of a credible deterrence regime against Iranian nuclear use. The United States could establish a nuclear umbrella over Middle East nations threatened by an Iranian nuclear weapon, but that would require defense treaties and greater U.S. commitment to an unstable region.
- Support for non-violent efforts at regime change in Tehran. Non-violent protests failed in 2009–2010 but might be revived. The prospects, however, are limited and the process could take years, during which Iran could develop nuclear weapons.
- Covert efforts to disrupt Iran's nuclear development.
- Independent Israeli airstrikes against nuclear facilities in Iran. Such strikes would probably not have an effective military result due to the distances involved, the number and type of Iranian targets, and Iranian air defenses. (If Israeli strikes take place in the context of a deal with Iran, it would cause a fundamental breach in relations between Israel and both the United States and the European Union.)
- U.S. airstrikes against multiple Iranian targets. Militarily, the results would likely be more effective than an Israeli strike, but hardened and deeply buried vaults housing centrifuges would be difficult to destroy. The results would likely be a costly military escalation, the risk of increased terrorism, and a diplomatic breech between the United States and Europe.

[41] Thomas Erdbrink, "Post-Deal Iran Asks if U.S. Is Still 'Great Satan,' or Something Less," *New York Times*, September 17, 2015.

Arabia and Egypt.[42] Congressional opponents of the agreement are threatening the imposition of new sanctions if Iran's regional behavior does not improve. Resolution of the different approaches between Khomeini and Rouhani will be critical to development of a more cooperative relationship between the United States and Iran.

Despite their many differences, Iran and the United States share an interest in the free flow of oil through the Strait of Hormuz. They also share an interest in successful implementation of the nuclear agreement, at least in the short run. Also, with the rise of ISIS, Iran and the United States are reluctantly cooperating to defeat a common enemy, even though leaders in both nations have been unwilling to formalize these cooperative arrangements. The next step in defeating ISIS may require U.S.-Iranian cooperation to transition the Damascus government from Assad to one with greater power-sharing arrangements. There is further room for improving U.S.-Iranian relations, which, if achieved, could affect the future of the Middle East.

Salafi Jihadists

Salafi jihadists were shown in the upper left-hand corner of Figure 3.1, indicating that they possess little global power and share no interests with the United States. This section will consider the two most prominent Salafi-jihadist groups: ISIS and al Qaeda.[43] Their differences with the United States are irreconcilable. In fact, their core ideology is a rejection of globalization and all Western values. Their conventional military capabilities are quite limited, but they nonetheless present a grave threat to U.S. global interests and to its homeland, though not an existential threat. Such groups could pose threats to international commerce, to U.S. interests abroad, and to American cities.[44] However,

---

[42] F. Gregory Gause III, *Beyond Sectarianism: The New Middle East Cold War*, Doha, Qatar: Brookings Doha Center, Analysis Paper No. 11, July 2014, p. 12.

[43] See Dobbins et al., 2015, pp. 34–35, for useful charts on the growth in the number of Salafi jihadists and in the number of their attacks.

[44] An August 4, 2015, article by Eric Schmitt in the *New York Times* argued that officials in Washington are split over their concern and priorities, with the Department of Home-

their long-term threat potential may be circumscribed by their lack of unity and their extremism, which has alienated many Muslims.[45]

ISIS has roots that go back to Tawhid wa'l Jihad in Jordan and then Afghanistan. Abu Musa al Zarqawi renamed it in late 2004 when he pledged *bayat* (allegiance) to Osama bin Laden. Its current leader, Abu Bakr al-Bagdadi, has set up a capital in Ar-Raqqah, Syria. It is the most vicious Sunni Islamist group in the Middle East, having been initially rejected by al Qaeda, the al-Nusra Front, and Ansar al-Islam for being too radical. It seeks a Salafist-jihadist caliphate in the Levant, including parts of Syria, Iraq, Turkey, Lebanon, Jordan, and Israel; it formally declared such a caliphate in June 2014. ISIS's supporters include Boko Haram, Jemaah Islamiya, al Qaeda in the Islamic Maghreb, and al Qaeda in the Arabian Peninsula. During the past year, ISIS has taken on some of the governance characteristics of a state in the area it controls, it has begun to decentralize authority to reduce the risk of leadership decapitation, and it has demonstrated its ability to conduct terrorist strikes from North Africa to Afghanistan.

ISIS surged onto the political map of the Middle East by taking advantage of political vacuums in Syria and Iraq. It has surprised Iraqi and Kurdish forces with its tactics and ferocity, and its leaders include many former mid-level military officers from Saddam Hussein's Ba'athist armed forces. ISIS has a sophisticated recruiting system that has attracted an estimated 12,000 fighters from some 50 countries, including about 2,000 from Western Europe—which raises the specter of homegrown terrorism.[46] ISIS employs excessive brutality and exhibits a strong desire for power. Violence is an end unto itself. How-

land Security focused on al Qaeda and the Defense Department focused on ISIS. See Eric Schmitt, "ISIS or Al Qaeda? American Officials Split Over Top Terror Threat," *New York Times*, August 4, 2015.

[45] See Seth Jones, "Islamic Jihadists: How Real a Threat?" *Christian Science Monitor,* March 30, 2015.

[46] Greg Miller, "New Rules for Visitors Exempt from Visas," *Washington Post*, November 4, 2014.

ever, it also offers recruits an answer to what some call "a yearning for a transcendental cause that liberal societies have trouble satisfying."[47]

Some have debated whether ISIS represents a direct threat to the United States and its allies. ISIS's first step is to purify Islam in its territory with a fundamentalist agenda that includes kidnapping, torture, rape, and execution of those considered apostates. It has committed systematic atrocities against Shi'ites and other minorities, including forcing young women into marriage and destroying ancient cultural sites. Its proof of concept extends to both civilians and military personnel caught in their web, including American, Japanese, Egyptian, and Jordanian hostages who were beheaded or burned alive in videotaped executions distributed worldwide via the Internet. Once ISIS completes this purification process and intimidates would-be enemies, it would presumably turn its attention to expansion. Its leader said in January 2014 that it would engage in "direct confrontation" with the United States.[48] Some 100 Americans are believed to be fighting under the ISIS banner and may represent a threat once they return home. Representative Michael McCaul (R-TX), chairman of the House Homeland Security Committee, argues the ISIS external operations are already under way.[49]

In September 2014, President Obama pledged to "degrade and ultimately destroy" the jihadist army of ISIS.[50] His plan includes organizing Sunni nations to join the effort; building a large international coalition; and employing targeted air strikes, financial measures, and special operations forces, but no ground combat troops engaged directly against ISIS.[51] Later that month, Obama sought to rally nations against ISIS during a speech at the United Nations. The United States has sub-

---

[47] Ross Douthat, "Our Thoroughly Modern Enemies," *New York Times*, August 23, 2014.

[48] Adam Goldman, "Officials: Islamic State Doesn't Pose an Immediate Danger to U.S.," *Washington Post*, September 11, 2014.

[49] Benjamin Bell, "ISIS Intent on Hitting West, McCaul Believes," *ABC News*, August 24, 2014.

[50] Spencer Ackerman, "Bullish Obama Vows to 'Degrade and Destroy' Islamic State," *The Guardian*, September 3, 2014.

[51] There are currently some 3,500 U.S. ground forces in Iraq serving as advisors.

sequently launched air strikes against ISIS concentrations in Iraq and Syria, provided food to Yazidi refugees, sent special operations forces to advise the Iraqi armed forces, and organized a coalition[52] to provide both air strikes and military assistance to the Iraqi Armed Forces and to the Kurdish Peshmerga.

Separate strategies may be needed to deal with ISIS in Syria and Iraq. In Iraq, the United States is struggling to coordinate with Iran while avoiding the appearance of doing so. As this is written, Iraqi army forces joined by Shi'a militias are expelling ISIS from Tikrit, with Mosul as the next goal. Turkey has joined the fight against ISIS in Syria with base support, air strikes, and an agreement to create a safe zone in Syria along their common border. Russia has complicated matters by deploying and using air power against both ISIS and more moderate Syrian opposition groups. In the end, this effort may not be enough. Estimates of the size of ISIS fighting forces vary widely, with an official estimate set at 20,000–30,000 fighters.[53] Large ground force operations plus a renewed "Sunni Awakening"—à la the "Anbar Awakening" of 2006—in Iraq plus a change in government in Damascus may be needed to completely dislodge this lethal group from both countries.

As this report was going to press, ISIS placed a bomb on a Russian airliner and attacked the streets of Paris. This is bringing together a strong U.S.-European-Russian-Iranian-Saudi coalition that has the power to defeat ISIS and find a new political solution to the Syrian conflict.

A catalogue of U.S. adversaries certainly cannot exclude al Qaeda and its affiliates, such as Jabhat al-Nusra. Since the death of Osama bin Laden in 2011, al Qaeda has dropped from the headlines but is now gaining strength in political vacuums such as Syria and Yemen. It remains a threat to the United States and Europe, has branched out to other countries, and works with more than a score of other Sunni Islamist groups to form a broader terrorist network. A new cell, called

---

[52] Including, among others, Australia, the United Kingdom, Jordan, Qatar, Saudi Arabia, Turkey, and the United Arab Emirates. See Helene Cooper and Mark Landler, "U.S. Mobilizes Allies to Widen Assault on ISIS," *New York Times,* August 26, 2014.

[53] Lucas Tomlinson, "'Stalemate': Size of ISIS Forces Unchanged Despite Year-Long Air Campaign," *FoxNews.com*, August 4, 2015.

the Khorasan group, has formed in Syria that seems intent on striking the United States and its partners. Some experts argue that the Khorasan group and al Qaeda's Syrian affiliate, the Nusra Front, present a greater terrorist threat than does ISIS.[54] Al Qaeda remains a major and growing threat. Affiliates in Syria, Somalia, Yemen, Libya, and West Africa have mounted major attacks and they are expanding their reach to the Indian subcontinent.[55]

Cooperation Among Potential Adversaries

Table 3.2 summarizes the governance models being offered by potential U.S. adversaries, their rivalries with U.S. partners, and their cooperation with other potential U.S. adversaries.

These governance models are quite different. Some stress nationalism, victimhood, and autocratic rule to achieve political order, economic growth, and common good over individual freedom (China,

Table 3.2
Potential Adversaries

	Model of Governance	Confrontation with U.S. Partners	Cooperation with Other Potential U.S. Adversaries
China	Elite caring for collective	Japan, Philippines, Taiwan	Russia, DPRK, Iran
Russia	Illiberal nationalism	Ukraine, Georgia, Baltic states, Poland	China, Iran
DPRK	Totalitarian, self-reliance	Republic of Korea, Japan	China, Iran
Iran	Shi'a theocracy	Israel, Saudi Arabia, Gulf Cooperation Council	Russia, China, DPRK
ISIS/al Qaeda	Sunni caliphate	Iraq, Turkey, Jordan, Lebanon	None

[54] Mark Mazzetti, Michael S. Schmidt, and Ben Hubbard, "U.S. Suspects More Direct Threats Beyond ISIS," *New York Times*, September 20, 2014.

[55] "Al-Qaida/Al-Qaeda (The Base)," *GlobalSecurity.org*, updated May 21, 2015.

Russia, and North Korea). Theocratic models have limited global appeal (Iran and ISIS). Given these differences, there is little chance that these models will merge into one coherent, global anti-liberal model that would threaten existing liberal democratic states, although all have authoritarian rule in common. Former U.S. Secretary of State Henry Kissinger has expressed concern that spheres of influence might develop "identified with particular domestic structures or forms of government."[56] The problem relates as much to the willingness of many of these nations to disavow the existing international rule of law, especially with regard to the use of force to expand national territory.[57] Several of these nations already cooperate with one another bilaterally when they have common interests.

The greatest danger to U.S. interests is the emergence of a close alliance between China and Russia, which could drive the international system back into a dangerous bipolarity. Both are autocratic governments taking steps to quash democracy movements at home and to cordon off separate national Internet systems, sometimes called "Splinternets." Both feel disadvantaged by history and, as a result, have territorial claims that conflict with their neighbors. Both are using hybrid tactics that mix force, intimidation, and salami-slicing techniques to uphold those claims. Both see the United States as trying to contain them and seeking some degree of regime change. Both are pursuing A2/AD capabilities. Both are members of the Shanghai Cooperation Organization. Russia and China cooperate on UN Security Council votes, energy, and arms sales—for example, Russia recently announced the sale of advanced S-400 air defense missiles to China. They hold military exercises together, even in the Mediterranean Sea. In May 2014, Putin and Chinese President Xi Jinping agreed to a long-term $400 billion gas deal that had been under negotiation for a decade. In October 2014, the two nations signed 38 trade, energy, financial, and defense agreements. The following month, they inked yet another

---

56 Henry Kissinger, "Henry Kissinger on the Assembly of a New World Order," *Wall Street Journal*, August 29, 2014a.

57 It is noted that the United States has also been accused of using force without proper international authority in the recent past.

agreement to boost energy cooperation and develop a second major route to supply Russian gas to China.[58] They have also agreed to pay their trade debts to each other in rubles and yuan, seeking to reduce the value of the dollar as a reserve currency.[59] During the May 2015 V-E Day celebration in Moscow, Xi was seated next to Putin, as most Western leaders boycotted the event.

Closer cooperation would benefit Russia, even though China presents a demographic threat to Siberia. Russia has turned its back on the West and now will have a difficult time repairing those ties. In October, Putin told Chinese Premier Li Keqiang: "We do have great plans . . . we are natural partners, natural allies, we are neighbors."[60]

China provides a good alternative for Russia, but from Beijing's standpoint, Moscow is not an ideal partner. During the Cold War, China saw itself treated like Russia's poor, country cousin; now the power relationship has reversed. China sees Russia as a declining power that is prepared to take excessive risks—risks that could get China into unwanted trouble. On Crimea, China refused to support Russian annexation and voted to abstain rather than support Russia on relevant UN Security Council resolutions. However, Russia and China have similar views of U.S. policies and could be driven into closer cooperation if the United States mismanages relations. That could create a more dangerous strategic situation.

These Adversaries Create Vulnerable Partners

The same partnerships that are vital for the United States to operate in the international system present a certain degree of risk. Most of the conflicts in which the United States has fought since the end of the Second World War were fought to protect partners; Korea, Viet-

---

[58] "China, Russia Sign Accord on Second Gas Route," *Associated Press*, November 9, 2014.

[59] "Russia and China Gang Up on U.S. Dollar as Economic Ties Deepen," *Moscow Times*, September 9, 2014.

[60] Michael Birnbaum, "Chinese Leader Signs Trade Deals with Russia," *Washington Post*, October 14, 2014a.

nam, and Kuwait are prime examples. Other wars were fought to protect a partner's neighborhood from humanitarian crises (e.g., Bosnia, Kosovo, and Libya). Only in a few cases has the United States gone to war to eliminate what appeared to be a direct threat to the United States: Panama in 1989 and Afghanistan in 2001. A U.S. decision to go to war has not required a firm defense treaty with the partner in question. In fact, in every case just cited, the United States went to war in the absence of a firm mutual defense treaty. So to maintain the benefits of its alliances and partnerships around the globe, the United States has paid a high price in blood and treasure over the past seven decades.

Today, if one considers the top five scenarios that might engage the United States in conflict, all five relate to protecting close allies and partners rather than protecting the United States from direct attack. Those five scenarios include (1) protecting South Korea from a North Korean attack, possibly in the context of a North Korean collapse; (2) defending an Asian treaty ally in the context of maritime disputes and conflict with China; (3) protecting the Baltic states from incursions by Russia; (4) dealing with a proliferating Iran (should the new agreement fail) that in the first instance would threaten Israel; and (5) protecting Turkey, Jordan, and Iraq from the spillover of civil war in Syria and from ISIS or allied groups. In the first three, conflict could be triggered by a firm defense treaty obligation. This is not to suggest that the commitments taken by the United States on behalf of its allies and partners are not worth the risk. In many ways, the United States' partners are its most important global asset. No U.S. adversary has as many friends, trading partners, investment agreements, or ties through diaspora communities, let alone treaty allies. This does suggest, however, that U.S. partners need to recognize these risks taken on their behalf by the United States and increase their commitment to contribute accordingly.

Back to Bipolarity?

The greatest long-term future risk for the United States may be a higher degree of coordinated action among adversaries. In the extreme, this could lead to a more bipolar—and potentially more unstable—world.[61]

During the 1990s, the international system was described as unipolar, with the United States as the sole remaining superpower. That moment passed in the following decade. Today, the international system is variously described as multipolar, polycentric, and nonpolar. These terms are used to describe the rise of emerging powers, including states, international organizations, and nonstate actors. Will some of these powers band together and cooperate against U.S. interests to form a more bipolar system?

One assessment of past international systems and the emerging post–Cold War system concluded that

> [f]ive international systems have existed since the birth of the United States.[62] We are now [1999] less than a decade into a sixth. Most of the previous systems, though Eurocentric, have tended to dominate world politics and they have become increasingly global. . . . Each of these five systems was initially multipolar rather than bipolar. Multipolarity made them more complex; movement in the system was relatively fluid; and state diplomacy could be flexible. . . . As each of the five previous systems matured, a degree of bipolarity set in. . . . Common interests bound the parties in all cases. . . . In every case it led to confrontation and in all but the last (the Cold War) it resulted in a system-changing war. Bipolarity was not the only factor that produced major conflict, but it provided a structure for it and appears to have made conflict more likely.[63]

---

[61] See Hans Binnendijk and Alan Henrikson, *Back to Bipolarity?* Washington, D.C.: National Defense University, Strategic Forum No. 161, May 1999.

[62] These five systems were (1) the Treaty of Utrecht to Waterloo, (2) the Congress of Vienna to the Crimean War, (3) the Rise of Germany to World War I, (4) the Interwar Period, and (5) the Cold War

[63] Binnendijk and Henrikson, 1999.

While the United States' adversaries are far from uniting to the point where the international system will return to a new form of bipolarity, this is a trend that needs to be watched carefully. A more bipolar world would be a serious setback for U.S. national security. Avoiding it should guide the United States' approach to China in particular.

Formidable Adversaries Make U.S. Retrenchment Difficult on Its Partners

The United States and its allies are facing a set of potential adversaries more challenging than at any time since the end of the Cold War. Europeans now refer to being surrounded by a ring of fire.[64] A policy of retrenchment would require the United States to set strict priorities based primarily on its own vital interests, not necessarily those of its partners. Some current U.S. commitments to allies and partners might need to be modified. And the United States would also need to offload many of its global security responsibilities to its partners.

It is unclear how the United States might set its priorities with regard to adversaries should it follow a path to retrenchment. Continuation of the pivot to Asia would be one option. However, given the conflict with ISIS and Russia's aggressive behavior, that would be a high-risk path.

Some of those challenges may be mitigated if the nuclear agreement with Iran is fully implemented and if progress can be made with China on maritime issues. If such efforts are successful, some of the U.S. defense burden might be lifted and some retrenchment might be possible. Even so, nervous partners will want assurances that the United States remains committed to providing military security in their region.

A general retrenchment approach might have been more feasible if Europe were indeed, in the words of President George H. W. Bush, "whole and free and at peace" and if significant U.S. military engagement in the Middle East were indeed at an end. However, given cur-

---

[64] Communicated to the author in private discussions with European officials.

rent global trends and new challenges posed by potential adversaries, a policy of retrenchment appears risky in the absence of diplomatic progress with China, Iran, or Russia.

A Strategy for Dealing with Potential Adversaries

All of these potential adversaries are autocratic and, to varying degrees, aggressive internationally. They are all challenging accepted international norms, rule of law, and governance models.

Most of these potential adversaries are cooperating with each other in efforts to frustrate U.S. policies; a higher degree of cooperation among them could form a more bipolar, hostile international order. Preventing collusion among them should be an important element of U.S. strategy. Lawrence Freedman has observed that "combining with others often constitutes the most astute strategic move; for the same reason, preventing opponents from doing the same can be as valuable."[65] If the United States were to follow this advice, it would focus on ways to prevent Russia and China from forming closer ties.

There are also dramatic differences among these potential adversaries; treating them alike would be a strategic mistake. This suggests a differentiated approach to these potential adversaries that would

- defeat ISIS, the foe that is most irreconcilable, the most brutal, and has the least capability
- maintain international pressure on al Qaeda and its affiliates through targeted operations
- deter the DPRK, a nation that is both dangerous and has no overlapping interests with the United States
- dissuade Russia from repeating its aggression using military preparedness and economic sanctions until it begins to modify its behavior
- constrain Iran's nuclear program and regional behavior

[65] Lawrence Freedman, *Strategy: A History*, New York: Oxford University Press, 2013, p. xi.

- engage with China, the nation that is potentially the most dangerous but also has significantly overlapping interests.

Dealing with China properly may be the most important of these policies. The key to improving relations with China will be finding an equitable settlement to China's maritime disputes and finding ways to convince China that the United States does not seek to contain China, without abandoning U.S. allies. A general approach might be to reform international institutions to give China a better seat at the table in exchange for a less confrontational Chinese policy on maritime claims. To accomplish this, the United States would need to engage in a deeper dialogue with China aimed at defusing the growing risk of confrontation.

CHAPTER FOUR

U.S. Constraints Limit Assertiveness

U.S. Attitudes Toward Global Responsibility

U.S. willingness to play an assertive leadership role is more circumscribed today than it was a decade ago. Recent polls demonstrate this public mood. Americans are exhausted from more than a decade of major wars in Afghanistan and Iraq. An estimated 52 percent of the American people now believe that the United States has "mostly failed" in Iraq,[1] while 49 percent believe the war in Afghanistan was a mistake (up from 10 percent at the outset of the war).[2]

A majority of Americans (53 percent) believe that the United States is less important and powerful in the world than it was ten years ago.[3] An astounding 80 percent of those surveyed in 2014 agreed that the United States should "not think so much in international terms but concentrate more on our own problems."[4] Other polls taken in 2014 indicated that between 40 and 47 percent of Americans felt that their country should be "less active" in world affairs.[5]

---

[1] Bruce Drake, "More Americans Say U.S. Failed to Achieve Its Goals in Iraq," Pew Research Center, June 12, 2014.

[2] Frank Newport, "More Americans Now View Afghanistan War as a Mistake," Gallup, February 19, 2014.

[3] Pew Research Center, "Public Sees U.S. Power Declining as Support for Global Engagement Slips," web page, December 3, 2013c.

[4] Max Fisher, "American Isolationism Just Hit a 50-Year High. Why That Matters," *Washington Post*, December 4, 2015.

[5] Brett LoGiurato, "There's Been a Dramatic Shift in American Attitudes Toward Foreign Policy, and Hawks Think They Have Their Moment," *Business Insider*, September 10, 2014.

In 2015, there has been a slight shift in public attitudes. A majority polled expressed concern about the lack of American assertiveness in negotiating with some potential adversaries.[6] Support for some increase in defense spending rose slightly, but 61 percent of those surveyed still believed defense spending is about right or too high.[7] Resistance to a larger U.S. global role remains. An August 2015 Associated Press–National Opinion Research Center (AP-NORC) poll found that 38 percent of Americans wanted a less active U.S. global role, 33 percent said the current role was about right, and only 28 percent wanted a more active U.S. role in the world.[8]

And yet, when things go badly internationally, the American people still want the United States to take bolder action. More than one-half of respondents in a January 2015 poll believed that President Obama is "not tough enough on foreign policy."[9] Some 61 percent in 2014 said they supported Obama's military operations against the Islamic State.[10] Finally, a September 2014 Chicago Council poll found that 83 percent of Americans surveyed wanted "strong U.S. leadership" in the world.[11] Yet even in the face of new terrorist threats, the American people want to meet those threats collaboratively with allies.

The American people have historically swung between support for intervention and isolationism. Now there appears to be a degree of schizophrenia embedded in these polls. They still want to lead but not necessarily in an assertive way. Also, they are less willing to pay the full cost in blood and treasure.

---

6 Lamont Colucci, "Voters Want America to Lead," *U.S. News and World Report*, March 18, 2015.

7 Justin McCarthy, "Americans Split on Defense Spending," Gallup, February 20, 2015.

8 Emily Swanson, "AP-NORC Poll: Terror Tops Americans' Foreign Policy Concerns," *Associated Press*, August 14, 2015.

9 Pew Research Center, "Obama Job Rating Ticks Higher, Views of Nation's Economy Turn More Positive," web page, January 14, 2015.

10 LoGiurato, 2014.

11 Liz Schrayer, "Election Forecast: World Events Shake Isolationist Trends," blog post, U.S. Global Leadership Coalition, October 31, 2014.

The greatest political divide is in the Republican Party.[12] The budget hawks of the Tea Party are much more isolationist than the traditionally assertive defense hawks of Republican Party leadership. Momentum in the Republican Party seems to be moving in the direction of the defense hawks. Divisions in the Democratic Party tend to focus more narrowly on the degree of military engagement needed to secure U.S. interests. If a more assertive approach is to prevail, it must overcome both the trend of American public opinion and elements in both political parties.

Shifting Global Defense Spending

Defense cuts are transatlantic. Table 4.1 summarizes a quarter century of defense spending by the United States, its largest defense partners, and its potential adversaries.

U.S. global dominance in defense spending is being challenged in the wake of its withdrawals from Iraq and Afghanistan and due to what might be called budget math. Spending on non-discretionary programs continues to push the overall U.S. national budget well above 20 percent of GDP, the limit of what U.S. taxes can finance. Without tax increases, the deficit continues to rise and pressure falls on discretionary budget items, including defense.[13] Significant U.S. defense cuts could therefore continue over the next few years even if sequestration constraints are lifted.

The Obama budget for fiscal year 2016 requests $585.3 billion for defense, an increase of $24.9 billion above fiscal year 2015. That includes a base budget of $534.3 billion and overseas contingency operations of $50.9 billion. The recently enacted two-year budget deal provides up to $607 billion for defense in 2016. Obama's request for the rest of the decade would modestly increase the base budget each year. These levels, however, are still a significant drop from the 2010

---

[12] In a recent AP-NORC poll, 38 percent of Republican respondents wanted a more active U.S. global role, while 44 percent wanted a less active U.S. role (Swanson, 2015).

[13] Robert J. Samuelson, "Partners in Budget Posturing," *Washington Post*, March 30, 2015.

Table 4.1
Comparative Defense Spending (in billions of constant 2011 U.S. dollars)

Country	1990	1995	2000	2005	2010	2013
United States	527.2	411.7	394.2	579.8	720.3	618.7
Partners						
France	70.5	65.0	61.8	65.1	66.3	62.3
Germany	71.7	53.2	50.6	47.0	49.6	49.3
Israel	13.6	12.5	14.5	15.9	16.0	16.0
Japan	47.8	56.8	60.3	61.3	59.0	59.4
South Korea	15.1	18.6	20.0	24.7	29.9	32.4
United Kingdom	58.8	48.4	48.0	58.2	62.9	56.2
South Asia						
India	18.8	19.6	27.7	36.1	49.2	49.1
Pakistan	4.4	5.0	4.8	6.4	6.6	7.6
Potential adversaries						
China	19.8	23.1	37.0	71.5	136.2	171.4
Russia	291.1	33.8	31.1	46.4	65.8	84.9
Iran	2.8	3.7	9.9	15.1	11.0	N/A

SOURCE: Stockholm International Peace Research Institute, undated.

NOTE: Reliable data for North Korea are unavailable, but its present level of defense spending is estimated to be around $10 billion.

spending level of over $700 billion, when operations in the Middle East were still at a high point.[14]

Force structure is being cut and readiness is in decline. For example, U.S. Army active duty end strength will drop from 570,000 in 2012 to a planned 450,000 in 2017. The Obama defense budget assumes that sequestration will be lifted and that some $115 billion

[14] Office of the Under Secretary of Defense (Comptroller), *Department of Defense Fiscal Year 2016 Budget Request*, Washington, D.C., February 2015, pp. 10–13.

in cuts in the base budget over five years will not take place.[15] Should sequestration not be lifted, the active duty Army would drop further to 420,000, the Marine Corps would drop from 202,100 in 2012 to 175,000, the Air Force would have to eliminate its entire fleet of KC-10 tankers, the Navy would have to mothball six destroyers and retire a carrier, and research and development would be cut dramatically.[16] Individual services are taking steps to protect their core assets, which has led to questionable force reductions in Europe.[17]

The United States still retains about 175,000 troops deployed permanently abroad.[18] This includes approximately 80,000 in Asia (50,000 in Japan and 28,000 in South Korea), 65,000 in Europe (including 38,000 in Germany, 11,000 in Italy, and 9,000 in Britain), and about 30,000 in the greater Middle East (9,800 in Afghanistan, 3,500 supporting anti-ISIS operations in Iraq, and 16,000 in and around the Persian Gulf). These forces provide reassurance to U.S. allies and deterrence against potential adversaries, but, in a time of major conflict, they would require significant reinforcement.

Chinese defense spending, in contrast, has increased by nearly a factor of ten during this period. Russia's defense spending collapsed after the demise of the Soviet Union, but it has increased dramatically over the past few years.

As U.S. defense spending declines and both Russian and Chinese spending increases, the defense budgets of principal U.S. allies have remained fairly constant over the past two decades. The top five U.S. allies now spend roughly the same on defense as do the top three

---

[15] See Lawrence Korb, Max Hoffman, and Katherine Blakeley, "A User's Guide to the Fiscal Year 2015 Defense Budget," Center for American Progress, April 24, 2014.

[16] U.S. Department of Defense, "DOD Releases Estimated Impacts of Sequestration-Level Funding Report," news release NR-187-14, Washington, D.C., April 15, 2014a.

[17] For example, the Army has decided to withdraw the 12th Combat Aviation Brigade from Europe at exactly the time when the mobility and firepower inherent in combat helicopters is most needed.

[18] See Annalisa Merelli, "Home Abroad: These Are All the Countries Where the US Has a Military Presence," *Quartz*, April 2, 2015. Note that these figures do not include all forces in each regional command, just those forward deployed on a permanent basis. For example, U.S. Pacific Command includes approximately 325,000 personnel.

U.S. potential adversaries.[19] At the global level, defense spending by the United States and its key allies remains dominant. In Asia and Europe, however, shifting trends may eventually provide new advantage to potential adversaries, especially if conflict is localized. This is particularly true in Europe, if the United States continues to downsize its force structure there despite Russian aggression.

Is the United States Overextended?

Conflict is possible with all potential adversaries discussed in the previous chapter. Further Russian military operations in Ukraine are unlikely to lead to a broader conflict unless they extend well beyond the Donbas area. However, an incident in one of the Baltic states could escalate quickly. Chinese-Japanese air or naval clashes near the Senkaku Islands could quickly develop into a broader confrontation. Iranian cheating on the nuclear deal could trigger a military response. Incidents along the Korean demilitarized zone or, more likely, in contested maritime areas could trigger a strong South Korean response. And the executions of James Foley, Steven Sotloff, and Japanese and Jordanian prisoners have already galvanized a U.S.-led coalition against ISIS.

The U.S. military will need to be prepared for all of these contingencies. In addition, RAND analyst Michael Mazarr has noted that adversaries are closing the technological gap with the United States and that geopolitical constraints on U.S. power are intensifying as the threat to the rules-based liberal international order grows.[20] Similarly, the 2015 National Military Strategy notes that: "The United States is the world's strongest power, enjoying unique advantages in technology, energy, alliances and partnerships, and demographics . . . however, these advantages are being challenged."[21] Recent press articles question

[19] Compare France, the United Kingdom, Japan, Germany, and South Korea with China, Russia, and Iran.

[20] Michael J. Mazarr, "Land Power and a Third Offset through a Wide-Angle Lens," *Warontherocks.com*, June 21, 2015.

[21] Joint Chiefs of Staff, 2015, p. 3.

the readiness of U.S. forces for sustained war.[22] Further, RAND analyst Timothy M. Bonds has recommended that the United States halt the downsizing of the Army until Russia's threats against the Baltic states have receded.[23] The Defense Department is pursuing a series of technological and operational innovations, called the "Third Offset," designed to use new technologies such as unmanned systems, long-range stealth aircraft and submarines, electromagnetic weapons, nanotechnology, and biotechnology to compensate for the Army's diminished size.[24] Operationally, several alternatives are under consideration to manage new A2/AD capabilities developed by potential adversaries (discussed in Chapter Six).

But a significant increase in U.S. defense spending to mitigate the risk posed by potential adversaries is unlikely. The 2014 Quadrennial Defense Review posited a force structure that has been called "win, deny."[25] Under this structure, the United States would seek to defeat an adversary in one theater and deny an aggressor its objective in a second theater by imposing unacceptable costs. This is a step down from previous strategies that were called "win, win" and "win, hold, win." The United States has what might be called a "one-and-a-half-theater" military strategy, but it faces potential adversaries in three theaters. David Ochmanek and colleagues concluded that "U.S. defense strategy is out of alignment with the resources that the nation has been devoting to the defense program."[26] If several conflicts were to take place simultaneously, the United States could become overextended.

---

[22] See, for example, Nancy A. Youssef, "Pentagon Fears It's Not Ready for a War with Putin," *The Daily Beast*, April 14, 2015.

[23] Timothy M. Bonds, *Limiting Regret: Build the Army We Will Need*, testimony presented before the National Commission on the Future of the Army, August 18, 2015.

[24] In this approach, the first offset was the development of nuclear weapons during the Eisenhower administration, and the second was development of information technologies and precision-strike weapons.

[25] U.S. Department of Defense, *Quadrennial Defense Review 2014*, Washington, D.C., 2014b, p. 22.

[26] David Ochmanek, Andrew R. Hoehn, James T. Quinlivan, Seth G. Jones, and Edward L. Warner, *America's Security Deficit: Addressing the Imbalance Between Strategy and Resources in a Turbulent World*, Santa Monica, Calif.: RAND Corporation, RR-1223-RC, 2015, p. 5.

This possible overextension will impact U.S. partners. Even in a second theater, U.S. partners may be more vulnerable than before and hence will need to do more to defend themselves—introducing a new burden sharing imperative. Before, these allies relied on the United States to carry most of the load while they did just enough to maintain a political commitment from Washington. Now, partners have a military imperative to be more serious about their own security because the U.S. military could become engaged in another theater and be unable to swing its forces quickly enough. The United States will need to consult closely with its partners to assure that their policies do not stimulate conflict. New consultative mechanisms may need to be established with potential adversaries to manage any crises that occur and to control escalation.[27]

U.S. Power to Coerce

Given the limitations on U.S. defense capabilities and public reluctance to use military force, there has been a growing impact of what might be called coercive power.[28] *Coercive power*, as defined here, uses means short of major military operations to force unfriendly states to do what they would rather not. Coercive power includes economic sanctions, arms embargoes, diplomatic sanctions, cyber operations, covert operations, resource manipulation, interdiction operations, military assistance to vulnerable partners, non-violent demonstrations, and political intimidation. It is an underrated yet increasingly valuable type of power. It depends heavily on the collaboration of U.S. partners.

The use of military power beyond exercises and freedom of navigation patrols will become increasingly difficult against China and Russia, except in extremis. That is because both nations will increasingly have the military technology to prevent U.S. forces from approaching their territory with armed force, through development of A2/AD

---

[27] See Kissinger, 2014a.

[28] This section is based on David Gompert and Hans Binnendijk, "The Power to Coerce," *U.S. News and World Report*, July 9, 2014b.

capabilities. In addition, both nations have nuclear arsenals that give pause to the use of conventional force. The use of conventional military force against a large nation such as Iran is also constrained because the American people dread another major military intervention in the greater Middle East. The use of hard power against ISIS, however, can be very effective.

Potential U.S. adversaries have become more adept at using coercive power. Russia uses covert paramilitary operations, resource manipulation, cyber attacks, and political intimidation. China uses fishing vessels and oil rigs to underline maritime claims, cyber theft, and political intimidation. Iran foments unrest around the Persian Gulf, uses proxies to threaten Israel and other enemies, and has threatened to close the Strait of Hormuz. Coercive power is at the heart of most international intrigue today.[29]

More attention, therefore, needs to be given to the United States' use of coercive power in dealing with countries like China, Russia, Iran, and North Korea. The United States has mastered economic and diplomatic sanctions and has used cyber operations effectively. Economic sanctions have a long and uneven history. They were successful, if slow, in freeing South Africans from apartheid and Eastern Europeans and Russians from communism. However, sanctions failed to halt nuclear proliferation in North Korea or deter rogue actors, such as Saddam Hussein. Sanctions are sometimes criticized as a way to "do something" when the United States lacks the will to use force, and as hurting ordinary citizens more than the governments they are intended to punish. Moreover, sanctions require international consensus and broad participation to work, which usually dilutes them.[30] Yet, sanctions have helped bring Cuba and Iran to the negotiating table, and they contributed to Putin's willingness to accept (if not fully implement) the Minsk II ceasefire agreement in Ukraine.

The United States has made improvements in designing sanctions that impose targeted financial costs on an adversary. Following the al Qaeda attacks of September 11, 2001, the U.S. Department of Trea-

---

[29] Gompert and Binnendijk, 2014b.

[30] Gompert and Binnendijk, 2014b.

sury and Intelligence Community honed their ability to find, track, squeeze, and shut down flows and holdings of money—thanks in part to the globalization of banking systems. It is getting harder and harder for states, groups, companies, and wealthy individuals to hide and move money, except under mattresses and in sacks. For lack of hard currency or credit, trade, investment and production suffers, as has been the case in Iran's energy sector.[31]

Owing to its prowess in information systems, the United States also has unrivaled and unprecedented coercive power to track and intercept shipments of illicit goods, to access and use cyberspace, to apprehend "high-value" individuals, to conduct discreet intelligence operations, and to provide rapid military assistance to vulnerable nations. The West used diplomatic coercion by ejecting Russia from the G-8 in response to the annexation of Crimea and cyber operations to hamper Iran's nuclear program.[32] As the United States becomes a major exporter of oil and liquefied natural gas, it may also be able to negate coercive efforts by the likes of Russia and Iran to manipulate fuel supplies as a weapon.[33]

Coercive power will have varying degrees of effectiveness for different countries. It may be most effective against Russia and Iran. China may have too much economic and technological prowess to be vulnerable to it. U.S. competition with Russia in particular may be determined by who can best harness and use coercive power. President Putin has used coercion vigorously, with what NATO calls hybrid warfare, to stay just under the West's red lines. He has repeatedly constricted gas supplies to bring Ukraine to heel and keep the European Union from opposing Russian policy. Along with low-grade paramilitary violence, Putin has conducted cyberwarfare operations against former Soviet states and has used political intimidation against Poland and the Baltic states. Yet, when it comes to alternatives to military force, the United

[31] Gompert and Binnendijk, 2014b.

[32] See David Sanger, "Obama Order Sped Up Wave of Cyberattacks Against Iran," *New York Times*, June 1, 2012.

[33] Gompert and Binnendijk, 2014b.

States has the stronger hand. It should play it strategically, selectively, shrewdly, and fiercely.

U.S. Energy Exports to Partners

Energy exports may become a new instrument of U.S. leverage. To the surprise of most Americans, hydraulic fracturing, or fracking, technology may turn the United States into a net energy exporter within the decade. It may be a net exporter of natural gas by 2018 and the world's top oil producer by 2020.[34] Supply is increasing and domestic demand is declining. While the United States may not be completely energy independent, its remaining sources, such as Canada, will be much more secure than its previous suppliers in the Middle East. That may shield the United States from some supply interruptions, but since energy markets are global, it will not isolate it from all risk. Under dire circumstances, the United States could contribute to a safety net for some of its partners and allies, who may be confronted with energy cutoffs initiated for political purposes.

The major political risk for U.S. partners in Europe is a cutoff of Russian gas supplies or major conflict in the Persian Gulf. Many Eastern European partners are highly dependent on Russian gas, especially during winter.[35] Russia is shifting its energy exports to Asia and might be in a better position to reduce flows to Europe. Several Eastern European U.S. allies are taking countermeasures to relieve this dependency. Lithuania has constructed a floating liquefied natural gas (LNG) terminal that could service all three Baltic countries. Poland is scheduled to open a new LNG terminal in 2015. Numerous other LNG terminals

---

[34] Bruce Jones, "Despite Growing Energy Independence, U.S. Cannot Escape Global Risks," *PlanetPolicy* blog, Brookings Institution, May 27, 2014.

[35] "How Much Europe Depends on Russian Energy," *New York Times*, September 2, 2014 (some examples: Slovakia, 98 percent; Lithuania, 92 percent; Poland, 91 percent; Bulgaria, 90 percent; Hungary, 86 percent; Finland, 76 percent; Czech Republic, 73 percent; Latvia, 72 percent; Estonia, 69 percent; Netherlands, 34 percent; Germany, 30 percent; Italy, 28 percent; Britain, 17 percent).

exist in Europe, but infrastructure for reverse flows to vulnerable countries needs improvement.

A major question will be whether the United States can indeed provide an emergency supply of energy for its vulnerable allies and in what time frame. It remains unclear what U.S. production levels will be five years from today, but it is unlikely that the United States will be able to provide significant energy exports to Europe any time soon. In addition, infrastructure for LNG facilities takes considerable time to build. Even if U.S. gas production rises quickly, its export to Europe is not a short-term solution. As U.S. export potential increases, global demand for energy will also increase by some 60 percent over the next two decades. Much of that increased demand will come from Asia. If market forces alone drive U.S. exports, there may not be an adequate supply for Europe.

The Impact of Budgetary Constraints and Public Attitude

Current constraints on the U.S. defense budget and public attitude toward greater engagement overseas place some limits on national security strategy. The type of assertive policy implemented a decade ago would be difficult to replicate without fundamental changes in both. Should major conflict involving the United States break out in more than one region of the world, the U.S. military would be stretched significantly. U.S. budgetary priorities and willingness to commit force could change in the face of increased threats from adversaries. But, absent a devastating incident such as 9/11, there is only limited evidence of a public desire to fundamentally change course. The American public still wants to concentrate primarily on domestic problems at the expense of international affairs, but it also expresses concern at signs of U.S. weakness. It wants to lead without fully paying the price.

The United States now faces the prospect of military conflict in three theaters. However, its Quadrennial Defense Review strategy of "win, deny" suggests a two- or even one-and-a-half-theater capability. That posture may be difficult to change, even under a different administration. As a result, the United States could be overextended if its allies do not share a greater portion of the burden. The nature of the burden-sharing imperative between the United States and its allies has therefore changed from a political requirement to a military one.[36]

While U.S. military capabilities are under stress, two more positive factors could provide some relief. The first is the maturation of coercive power. The second is the potential for U.S. energy independence and the positive effect that may have on U.S. partners. Upon examination, coercive power may have a greater positive effect in the midterm than would U.S. energy independence.

This conclusion does not mean that the United States should not assert its interests or its values internationally. It does mean that, in doing so, the United States must recognize its constraints and seek greater international collaboration whenever it can.

---

36 Joint Air Power Competence Center, 2014b, pp. 139–147.

CHAPTER FIVE

European Partners and the "Free Rider" Problem

Paradigm Lost

During the 25 years since the fall of the Berlin Wall, Europe has developed a paradigm based on the proposition that European integration, peace, and prosperity are the new normal. That notion was formalized in the 1993 Maastricht Treaty that created the European Union. Many in Europe had accepted Francis Fukuyama's now outdated notion that liberal democracy had become the permanent natural order. Direct threats to Europe seemed limited to transnational problems that did not require large defense budgets to manage. This paradigm has now been badly shaken in the past half decade, with major Islamist terrorist attacks on European capitals, the euro crisis, Russian revanchism, violence and massive migration stemming from the Arab Spring, right-wing political movements in Europe, and defense fatigue from contributions to U.S. operations in Iraq and Afghanistan.

Europe is now divided between the east and west on security issues and between the north and south on economic issues. Eastern Europeans lived through Russian domination during the days of the Warsaw Pact and do not want to repeat the experience. These countries feel directly threatened by Putin's aggressiveness, though minority right-wing parties in Greece, Hungary, and elsewhere have argued that Russia is their natural ally. Citizens in Southern and Western Europe have increased their focus on the surge in refugees and immigrants landing on their shores as a result of conflicts and privation ranging from Syria to Kashmir and from Libya to Somalia.

On the economic front, the 2008 global recession is not over in Europe, with unemployment still above 11.5 percent. Southern Europe was particularly hard-hit. Northern Europe became the continent's creditor, dictating sometimes draconian austerity measures in exchange for debt relief. As the U.S. economy has recovered from that powerful recession, European economies continue to stumble with near-zero growth rates in most of the euro zone and potential default in Greece.[1] Support for the EU itself is in dramatic decline, with favorable perceptions declining to 43 percent in Britain, 41 percent in France, and 33 percent in Greece.[2] The perception that the EU is incompetent and out of touch with its citizens has helped fuel a rise in right-wing anti-immigrant and anti-EU sentiment throughout Europe. The latest European parliamentary elections enhanced the power of many extremist parties, which now number some 25 to 30 percent of the European Parliament and have seated overtly anti-Semitic lawmakers. A number of these nationalistic parties have also expressed a fondness for Putin's nationalistic policies and approval of his annexation of Crimea. The recent European migration crisis is expected to make this problem worse.

This shattered post–Cold War paradigm leaves Europe in a difficult position. European leaders are beginning to appreciate the dangerous security situation that confronts them, but they do not have enough euros to pay the needed defense bills. Their dependency on Russian trade and energy imports constrains their willingness to use economic sanctions.

To deal with this lost paradigm, Europe will now rely on both a set of established national leaders and a set of newly appointed European institutional leaders. Chancellor Angela Merkel of Germany champions a federalist approach for Europe, while, at the other end of the spectrum, the UK's David Cameron has promised a public referendum in 2017 on whether his country should remain engaged with

---

1 Liz Alderman and Alison Smale, "Divisions Grow as a Downturn Rocks Europe," *New York Times*, August 29, 2014.

2 Pew Research Center, "The New Sick Man of Europe: the European Union," web page, May 13, 2013a.

expanding EU federalism. Four new EU and NATO leaders are Germany's choice for the European Commission Presidency and arch-federalist Jean-Claude Juncker of Luxembourg; European Council President Donald Tusk of Poland; Federica Mogherini of Italy, head of the EU's External Action Service; and NATO Secretary General Jens Stoltenberg of Norway. Together, they represent the broad range of political views, experience, and geographic diversity that will be needed to contend with Europe's new situation. However, there are differences of opinion. Cameron, Stoltenberg, and Tusk all take a hard line on Russian revanchism, while Merkel and Mogherini have tended toward a more conciliatory approach with Russia.[3] That European balance may be needed to help find a new relationship with Russia somewhere between a new Cold War and strategic partnership.

Vulnerable Partners

From a security perspective, Europe is home to a number of vulnerable nations:[4]

- Russia has troops in several non-NATO countries (including Georgia, Ukraine, and Moldova), two of which have formal partnerships with NATO.
- Russia also seeks to intimidate NATO members in the Baltic states and Poland. It has declared its interest in protecting the Russian-speaking minorities in the Baltic states, strengthened its military capabilities near Russian borders with those states, and staged snap exercises designed to intimidate them. Despite NATO countermeasures, the Baltic states remain highly vulnerable to intervention and a possible land grab.

3 Tusk is expected to work to keep the UK in the EU and to revive the EU's Eastern Partnership. See Judy Dempsey, "What Tusk and Mogerini Mean for Europe," *Strategic Europe* blog, Carnegie Europe, September 1, 2014.

4 As a result of these vulnerabilities, Dobbins et al., 2015, concludes that "nowhere is the gap between U.S. security commitments and regional posture more pronounced than in Europe" (p. 28).

- Finland and Sweden are important NATO partners, but as nonmembers they remain vulnerable to Russian harassment.
- Chaos and the ongoing jihadist insurgency in much of the Middle East has increased the terrorist threat in Western Europe and increased the flow of refugees, particularly to Italy and economically vulnerable Greece. Homegrown terrorism stimulated by jihadist movements in Syria is a growing threat. Turkey, in particular, feels the direct impact of ISIS, the Syrian civil war, and the resulting surge in refugees.
- If Iran continues with its nuclear and missile programs, southwestern Europe will be within range of Iranian missiles.

Three of the most militarily vulnerable nations are not members of the NATO alliance: Ukraine, Georgia, and Moldova.[5] In so-called frozen conflicts, Russia has carved out pieces of its neighbors' territory where Russian-speakers are concentrated and have autonomous or independent entities. In Ukraine, Russia annexed Crimea and suggested that it might support a new sovereign entity called Novorossiya, which would include portions of Ukraine north of the Black Sea.[6] In Georgia, Russia occupied and has sought independent status for Abkhazia and South Ossetia. In Moldova, Russian troops control an eastern strip called Transnistria (or the Pridnestrovian Moldavian Republic). Some believe that Putin's strategic plan is to eventually connect the territories of these breakaway regions directly to Russia.

The EU set out to negotiate association agreements with all three countries, which created the impression in Russia of a zero-sum game with the Moscow-backed Eurasian Customs Union. By offering Ukraine an inadequate financial package, the EU contributed to former President Viktor Yanukovych's rejection of the association agreement and the subsequent Maidan protests. Germany, France, and

---

[5] Ukraine and Georgia are formal NATO partners. Moldova is not, but it has very close ties with Romania, a NATO member.

[6] *Novorossiya* is a historical term used by the Russian Empire, beginning in 1764, to describe a new province that extended across what is now southern Ukraine and the former Moldavian region of Bessarabia.

Poland then took steps to make the association agreement less of a zero-sum arrangement. Association agreements were signed with Ukraine, Georgia, and Moldova in June 2014. However, Putin has not given up and is attempting to block implementation of the agreements. In a letter to Josef Manuel Barroso, President of the European Commission, in late September, he demanded the reopening of the negotiations on the agreement and threatened to take "immediate and appropriate retaliatory measures" if Ukraine seeks to implement the agreement.[7]

NATO has had formal commissions that provide for consultations and military cooperation with Ukraine and Georgia. In the run-up to the 2008 NATO summit in Bucharest, U.S. President George W. Bush pushed hard for the Alliance to grant Ukraine and Georgia pre-membership status by negotiating Membership Action Plans (MAPs). These MAPs were viewed by many, especially the Russian leadership, as precursors to NATO membership. France and Germany, however, opposed granting Ukraine MAP status, fearing that it would antagonize Russia and lead to a deterioration of relations, and they succeeded in blocking efforts to grant MAPs to Ukraine and Georgia. However, the communiqué issued at the end of the summit by the NATO heads of state and governments stated that Ukraine and Georgia would one day be admitted to NATO, although no specific date or timetable was mentioned. Thus, from Moscow's point of view, the outcome was even worse than the Russian leadership had expected. While Ukraine and Georgia had been denied MAPs, they had been given a formal commitment that they would one day be full members of the NATO alliance. However, in the aftermath of the Russian invasion of Georgia in 2008, the issue of NATO membership for both Ukraine and Georgia was put on indefinite hold. While the door to Ukrainian and Georgian membership in NATO remains open rhetorically, in practice membership for both countries has been relegated to the back burner.

Following Russia's annexation of Crimea and the Russian-backed separatist uprising in eastern Ukraine, Germany and France negotiated a ceasefire agreement between Kiev and Moscow (Minsk II.) However,

---

[7] Peter Spiegel, "Putin Demands Reopening of EU Trade Pact with Ukraine," *Financial Times*, September 26, 2014.

the Minsk II agreement is violated daily. The United States, Germany, and France have cooperated closely in maintaining economic sanctions on Russia as an incentive to implement Minsk II, but American and German publics differ significantly over the mechanisms needed to provide longer-term security for Ukraine. Germans favor providing economic aid (71 percent versus 62 percent of Americans) while Americans place greater emphasis on providing military aid (46 percent versus 19 percent of Germans) and in bringing Ukraine into the NATO alliance (62 percent versus 36 percent of Germans).[8]

The second group of vulnerable European nations includes NATO members: the Baltic states, Poland, and Turkey. The Baltic states were invaded and integrated into the Soviet Union against their will at the beginning of World War II. Immediately after the war, Stalin launched a Russification program that sent ethnic Russians to live in all three states. Currently, there are about one million ethnic Russians living in the Baltic states, with strong concentrations in cities like Narva and Riga.[9] Upon achieving independence in 1991, Estonia and Latvia required ethnic Russians who arrived after 1940 to learn the national language before attaining citizenship. Resentment continues among Russian-speakers in both countries, and Putin's policy of protecting Russian-speakers everywhere may portend efforts to create instability. The Baltic states watch events in Ukraine with trepidation. Unlike Georgia, Moldova, and Ukraine, the Baltic states are already members of both NATO and the European Union. NATO has made significant efforts, including at the recent Wales Summit, to create a Readiness Action Plan (RAP) to provide them with military assistance if a need arises.[10] President Obama visited Estonia before the Wales Summit to underscore the U.S. determination to underwrite Baltic security.

---

[8] Katie Simmons, Bruce Stokes, and Jacob Poushter, "NATO Publics Blame Russia for Ukrainian Crisis, but Reluctant to Provide Military Aid," Pew Research Center, June 10, 2015.

[9] About one-quarter of the Latvian and Estonian populations are of Russian origin.

[10] This plan would create a small, very highly ready joint force for deployment within 5–7 days; prepositioned military stocks, including in the Baltic states themselves; contingency plans for Russian hybrid operations; snap exercises; and other measures designed to deter

Poland is more critical of Russia than any other European nation. It twice agreed to accept U.S. missile defense interceptors knowing that Moscow would react harshly. It is one of the few NATO members that is devoting 2 percent of GDP to defense. During a 2014 visit to Warsaw, President Obama promised a $1 billion European Reassurance Initiative for eastern NATO nations, reinforcing the U.S. commitment to Poland.

Turkey is most affected by the Syrian civil war and the emergence of ISIS; it hosts about 1.2 million Syrian refugees.[11] The Syrian military occasionally threatens border areas. NATO has deployed Patriot air defense batteries from three countries to help Turkey defend itself against Syrian aircraft and missiles that have crossed into its airspace.

Finland and Sweden are in a third category of potentially vulnerable European states. Both nations are EU members, but they are traditionally militarily non-aligned and are only partners, rather than full members, of NATO. Russia has recently conducted harassing military flights and submarine patrols as a warning to them to eschew full NATO membership, but this appears to have backfired and given the debate about possible NATO membership new momentum. Still, membership seems unlikely in the near future. Both countries have signed memoranda of understanding with NATO that allow the Alliance to use military infrastructure should Sweden and Finland come under attack. Military interoperability will also be increased and a new Partnership Interoperability Initiative will further strengthen their ties to the Alliance.[12] The NATO alliance would be much stronger militarily and politically if these two states became members. The key tactical question is how best to encourage them to join without creating a

---

Russia. The United States also has about 300 troops deployed on a rotational basis in each of the Baltic states and in Poland. Baltic air policing missions have been reinforced.

[11] Stuart Williams, "Turkey Calls for Help with Syrian Refugees as Tensions Rise," *The Daily Star* (Lebanon), August 15, 2014.

[12] Hans Binnendijk, Debra Cagan, and Andras Simonyi, "NATO Enlargement and Enhanced Partnership: The Nordic Case," in Daniel S. Hamilton, Andràs Simonyi, and Debra Cagan, eds., *Advancing U.S.-Nordic-Baltic Security Cooperation: Adapting Partners to a New Security Environment*, Washington, D.C.: Center for Transatlantic Relations at Johns Hopkins University, School of Advanced International Studies, 2014.

domestic backlash that would undercut the movement toward closer defense cooperation.

Europe would also be vulnerable to Iranian nuclear weapons and missile programs if the current nuclear agreement with Iran fails to be implemented properly. The European Phased Adaptive Approach is the U.S. contribution to a larger NATO ballistic missile defense program aimed at addressing this threat. It is designed to meet shorter-range threats first and to expand defenses in three phases, should the threat grow. Standard Missile III interceptors are to be deployed at sea, in Romania, and, by 2018, in Poland. Turkey has accepted the deployment of a U.S. ballistic missile defense radar system on its soil. A NATO system funded by all NATO allies, called the Active Layered Theatre Ballistic Missile Defense program, will provide command and control. Many European nations are contributing their own shorter-range missile interceptors and some will provide additional radar systems. However, the United States is providing most of the funding for a program that is now exclusively designed for European defense. Some greater burden sharing may be needed.

Declining Capabilities and Will in Europe

A drop in European defense spending over the past two decades has degraded capabilities. Table 5.1 shows a slow but steady decline in European defense spending relative to GDP since the end of the Cold War, a response to the new European paradigm discussed previously.[13] The United States, in contrast, reduced defense spending during the peaceful decade of the 1990s, but responded to the 9/11 attacks with a major defense effort. These trends also reflect U.S. global responsibilities. With the growing vulnerabilities in Europe vis-à-vis Russia, European defense spending trends will need to be reversed.

---

[13] As seen in Table 5.2 later in this chapter, European defense spending in constant dollar terms has remained remarkably steady for three decades. The problem is that Europe's economic growth during that period did not result in a commensurate increase in defense spending.

Table 5.1
Percentage of GDP Spent on Defense

	1990–1994	1995–1999	2000–2004	2005–2009	2010	2013
Europe[a]	2.5	2.1	1.9	1.8	1.7	1.6
United States	4.5	3.2	3.3	4.4	5.3	4.4

SOURCE: NATO, "Financial and Economic Data Relating to NATO Defence," press release, PR/CP(2014)028, February 24, 2014a.

[a] European members of NATO.

Europe's largest militaries took some of the biggest cuts during the past two decades. For example, German defense spending as a percentage of GDP fell from 2.1 percent to 1.3 percent; France from 3.3 percent to 1.9 percent; the United Kingdom from 3.6 percent to 2.4 percent; Italy from 2.0 percent to 1.2 percent; and Turkey from 2.8 percent to 1.8 percent.[14] Additional cuts have been projected during the next several years. Many of the previous cuts were not coordinated in advance with NATO defense planners, so redundancies exist in some areas and major gaps exist in others.[15]

With regard to military capabilities, the first defense reductions were horizontal, in that they cut across the board, creating a more hollow force. Later cuts tended to be more vertical, with nations removing entire capabilities from their force structure. The net effect was to curtail training and reduce readiness, postpone or cancel procurement essential to future operations, reduce force structure significantly, hamper deployability and sustainability, and abandon plans for force reconstitution. This led former U.S. Secretary of Defense Robert Gates to opine that such declines would make NATO's future "dim if not dismal."[16]

---

[14] NATO, 2014.

[15] Guillaume Lasconjarias, "NATO's Land Forces: Losing Ground," American Enterprise Institute, June 4, 2014.

[16] Tom Shanker, "Defense Secretary Warns NATO of 'Dim' Future," *New York Times*, June 10, 2011.

Public will to fight in most western and southern European countries is weak, even in the case of defending an ally against armed attack. A June 2015 Pew Research Center poll showed that 58 percent in Germany, 53 percent in France, and 51 percent in Italy would not be willing to use armed force to defend treaty allies if they got into a serious military conflict with Russia. Compare these response rates with the 37 percent found in both the United States and Britain. One reason for this limited willingness to defend eastern NATO allies appears to be that about 68 percent of the European population polled believes that the United States would use force to defend a NATO ally against Russia.[17]

Four mitigating factors balance this otherwise negative story. First, in 2013, European members of NATO spent about $300 billion on defense, a still considerable amount if used efficiently.[18] Second, U.S. defense spending during the past decade was heavily tilted toward sustaining ground-based stability operations in Iraq and Afghanistan, and U.S. defense spending is now in steep decline as those operations seek to wind down. Third, most European forces during this period transformed from larger conscription forces to smaller but more modern and responsive volunteer forces. Those mobile forces gained valuable experience in Afghanistan. Finally, at the recent Wales Summit, European heads of state made commitments to reverse these trends with agreed movement toward the NATO defense-spending goal of 2 percent of GDP. However, the process of reversal could easily take more than a decade.

Nonetheless, the story remains one of diminished European defense capabilities as vulnerabilities grow. A 2012 RAND study drew three dramatic conclusions about the impact of two decades of defense cuts:

- The units of account for European ground forces will be battalion battle groups and brigade combat teams, not full-strength divisions and corps.

---

[17] Simmons, Stokes, and Poushter, 2015.

[18] Stockholm International Peace Research Institute, undated.

- If NATO Europe got involved in a major operation in the Mediterranean, it would not likely have the reserve capacity to address . . . a higher-risk contingency.
- In light of the collective NATO experience during its protracted large-scale counterinsurgency operation in Afghanistan, NATO Europe will have neither the will nor the capability to maintain a multi-brigade expeditionary force over a long distance from Europe for a multiyear peace-enforcement mission.[19]

Land forces have borne the brunt of the force reductions.[20] A 2013 RAND study pursued this assessment by looking at the British, French, and German armies and made the following basic conclusions:

- The British Army has been the most adversely affected by the Iraq and Afghanistan missions. Its military equipment has been heavily used and much of its defense budget has been spent on current operations. Modernization schedules have been postponed. Its new family of medium-armored vehicles may not enter service for another decade due to diversion of funds. Expenditures on nuclear submarines for deterrence and on carriers for force projection have cut into funds for ground forces. British planners want to restore the army's full spectrum of capabilities and will accept large cuts in force size and tiered readiness to accomplish this. The UK's future contributions to coalition ground force operations will be measured in brigades, not divisions.
- The French Army is less affected by the Afghanistan mission. It too is dedicated to maintaining a full spectrum of ground capabilities. A vehicle modernization program is well under way. However, unlike the United Kingdom, France is more skeptical that technological enhancements can substitute for reduced force structure.

---

[19] F. Stephen Larrabee, Stuart E. Johnson, John Gordon IV, Peter A. Wilson, Caroline Baxter, Deborah Lai, and Calin Trenkov-Wermuth, *NATO and the Challenges of Austerity*, Santa Monica, Calif.: RAND Corporation, MG-1196-OSD, 2012, p. xvi.

[20] Lasconjarias, 2014.

- The German Army has moved to an all-volunteer force and is retaining more heavy forces than France or Britain. Germany's commitment to the combined-arms maneuver warfare end of the capability spectrum is weak and it is focusing more on stability operations.[21]

Airpower has also suffered under budget reductions. A recent NATO Joint Air Power Competence Center study concluded "the lengthy run of defense cuts is starting to impact Air and Space Power capabilities and jeopardize its continued effectiveness . . . recent operations revealed shortages in a broad range of enabling capabilities."[22]

European capacity and willingness to sanction Russia is also affected by both trade and energy dependency. European bilateral trade with Russia is about $325 billion annually, with Europe running a sizable deficit. Russia is Europe's third largest trading partner, while Europe is Russia's largest. Europe primarily exports machinery, transport equipment, chemicals, medicines, and agricultural products, and imports natural gas and oil. Europe imports about one-third of its gas from Russia, with nations to the east even more heavily dependent.[23] The European Union also provides about 75 percent of Russia's foreign direct investment. Therefore, the capacity of the EU to harm the Russian economy is great, but so is Russia's ability to retaliate.

In a renewed show of European determination and in coordination with the United States, in 2014–2015 the EU implemented several

---

[21] Michael Shurkin, *Setting Priorities in the Age of Austerity: British, French, and German Experiences*, Santa Monica, Calif.: RAND Corporation, RR-222-A, 2013, pp. xi–xii.

[22] Joint Air Power Competence Center, *Present Paradox—Future Challenge*, Kalkar, Germany: North Atlantic Treaty Organization, March 2014a, p. 129.

[23] Lithuania, Estonia, Latvia, and Finland are 100-percent dependent on Russia for natural gas; Bulgaria, Slovakia, and the Czech Republic are more than 85-percent dependent; Poland, Greece, Hungary, Slovenia, and Austria are all between 55- and 65-percent dependent; Germany and Belgium are more than 40-percent dependent. See Clingendael International Energy Programme, *Russian Gas Imports to Europe and Security of Supply*, fact sheet, undated.

sets of economic sanctions to punish Russia's activities in Ukraine.[24] France—which has given high priority to international arms sales in the past—finally agreed to suspend the sale of two *Mistral*-class helicopter carriers to Russia in November 2014.[25]

To assess the broader implications of defense cuts, war weariness, and economic dependencies on Europe's capabilities and will, in June 2014 RAND hosted a focus group of about 20 U.S. experts on European defense matters. The group was asked to rate the capabilities and will of various European countries and regional groups. Based on these ratings and focus group discussions, the assembled American experts came to the following conclusions:

- Many European nations are underperforming when it comes to both capabilities and will to act.
- Germany received relatively low marks across the board for both capabilities and will, given its economic strength and leadership position in the European Union.
- Nonetheless, there are pockets of strength in Europe that need to be enhanced and better organized.
- France and the United Kingdom remain the most capable and willing partners for the United States, but their defense budget cuts will harm their ability to contribute consistently in the future.
- Norway, Sweden, Finland, Belgium, the Netherlands, and Luxembourg tend to have enough will to act, but bring relatively little military capability with them.
- The Visegrad states are badly divided, with Poland taking what some have called alarmist positions on Russia while Hungary and, to a lesser degree, Slovakia and the Czech Republic unwilling to support a tough line against Moscow.
- There is less interest in Northern Europe in engaging in crisis-management operations.

---

[24] Laurence Norman and William Mauldin, "EU to Put New Sanctions on Russia," *Wall Street Journal*, September 11, 2014.

[25] Maïa de la Baume, "French Defense Minister Says Russia May Never Receive Mistral Warships," *New York Times*, December 5, 2014.

- Mediterranean countries, including Turkey, tend to have more capability than expected and, not surprisingly, focus more on crisis management to their south.
- Most nations remain interested in cooperative security (i.e., developing partnership capacity, arms control, nonproliferation, coordination with other international organizations, regional security arrangements).
- The allies to the east that are the most threatened also tend to have little relative power to exercise; their defense budgets are surprisingly low.
- European trade with Russia is about a dozen times that of the United States. Many European nations are heavily dependent on Russian energy, so the use of coercive power, such as economic sanctions, is more painful for them; they are reluctant to use this potentially powerful instrument.[26]

Three Pivotal Partners: The United Kingdom, Germany, and Turkey

The future strength of the NATO alliance will be most decisively affected by the directions taken by three nations: the United Kingdom, Germany, and Turkey.

United Kingdom: The May 2015 elections in the United Kingdom could set in motion events that would negatively impact this top U.S. NATO ally, possibly leading to what some refer to as "small England."[27]

---

[26] These conclusions have not been published previously. They are based on a working group discussion and questionnaire organized by the author together with Chris Chivvis and Richard Solomon.

[27] See Griff Witte and Dan Balt "Britain Faces Crucial Choices," *Washington Post*, May 10, 2015; Anne Applebaum, "The End of Britain as We Know It," *Washington Post*, May 11, 2015; E. J. Dionne Jr., "David Cameron's Wizardry," *Washington Post*, May 11, 2015; and Kathrin Bennhold, "A Chasm Divides Leaders of a Kingdom Still United," *New York Times*, May 11, 2015.

The unexpectedly solid victory of the Conservative Party may have a stabilizing impact on the British economy, but other aspects of the election could have severe consequences for the United States. The first consequence is the dramatic victory of the Scottish Nationalist Party (SNP), which took 56 of 59 Scottish seats in Parliament—at the expense, primarily, of the Labor Party. The Labor Party has subsequently shifted further to the left. The SNP leadership will now press for greater fiscal autonomy (taxes and budgets) and will seek to shift Scotland in a more progressive economic direction, as Prime Minister Cameron continues with more conservative economic policies. Creating widely diverse fiscal policies in one monetary system has not worked well in the EU and is not likely to work well in the UK. The probable result will be renewed pressure for another Scottish referendum on independence. The recent referendum lost by a wide margin, but it may succeed the next time.

A second consequence of the May election is a more certain prospect for a referendum in 2017 on the UK's continued membership in the European Union. While the anti-EU UK Independence Party took only one seat in parliament, it did win nearly 17 percent of the vote. Cameron has said that he will try to renegotiate the UK's relationship with the EU before that referendum, and he has traveled to Berlin, Paris, Warsaw, and The Hague to gather support for that effort. German Chancellor Merkel and other European leaders showed some willingness to compromise, but a UK exit from the EU is certainly possible.

In addition to these two possible acts of political separation, the need for economic austerity has given rise to the concern that British defense spending will continue to decline. Prime Minister Cameron addressed this concern in July 2015 by—surprisingly—pledging to maintain British defense spending at 2 percent of GDP. This spending will be used primarily to update the UK's submarine-based nuclear deterrent, build two new aircraft carriers, purchase F-35s, and modernize its conventional equipment, which has been heavily used in Iraq and Afghanistan. There will be continued pressure to contract the size of UK ground forces. Nonetheless, Cameron also suggested that the ongoing Strategic Defense and Security Review should consider spending more on efforts to fight ISIS.[28]

If the United Kingdom leaves the European Union or divides, the consequences could be severe. Britain's focus during the years immediately following either scenario would be on domestic issues. London's ability to contribute to joint military operations would be limited. England might lose its submarine base in Scotland, just as it seeks to modernize its nuclear deterrent. Finally, British influence in EU decision-making would disappear.

Germany: Germany holds the keys to a surge in European defense capabilities and willingness to act. It could easily spend an additional $20 billion or more on defense each year, close to the 2 percent of GDP target. Its current defense spending level is at about 1.3 percent of GDP, which may decline this year. This makes Germany, the fourth-largest economy in the world, one of Europe's largest free riders. Equally important, Germany has shied away from contributing forces to some key NATO operations, with the Libya operation being the most visible. A June 2015 Pew Research Center poll found that 58 percent of Germans said Germany should not use military force to defend NATO allies who are engaged in serious military conflict with neighboring Russia.[29] Germany was initially slow to agree to economic sanctions against Russia for its annexation of Crimea, but eventually did implement sanctions and brought the rest of the EU along. It provided significant support to ISAF and eventually joined three rounds of European sanctions against Russia over Putin's operations in Ukraine. German defense spending is unlikely to increase significantly in the near term, but there are signs that it is more willing to participate in future NATO operations. The cost of absorbing the recent flood of Syrian refugees will probably stall any increase in German defense spending for several years.

---

[28] Stephen Castle, "British Premier Urges Military to Spend More to Fight ISIS," *New York Times,* July 13, 2015.

[29] Simmons, Stokes, and Poushter, 2015. Response rates to the same question in other NATO countries: United States (37 percent), UK (37 percent), Poland (34 percent), France (53 percent), and Italy (51 percent).

There are multiple potential explanations for this German reluctance:

- Germany still recalls its World War II history and is hesitant to become a nation with strong military capabilities again.
- A reunified Germany feels more secure than at any time in the past century and does not feel directly threatened by events in the greater Middle East. Events in Ukraine have disrupted, but not undone, that feeling of security.
- Publications on *Putin verstehen*, or "understanding Putin," have become a cottage industry in Germany.
- Germany has been able to finance significant European debt during the euro crisis and still maintain a budget surplus. Its focus is on European economic recovery, preservation of the euro zone through austerity, and absorbing a million new refugees. Additional German defense spending now would, in Berlin's view, break the bank.
- Germany is reliant on Russia for energy imports (gas: 38 percent; oil: 35 percent; coal: 25 percent)[30] and Russia is Germany's fifth-largest export market, so economic sanctions against Russia are painful for Germany. German businesses have urged Chancellor Merkel to halt sanctions.[31]
- German public opinion has lost trust in the United States as the leader of NATO. Germans' "favorable opinion" of the United States fell from 60 percent in 2002, just after 9/11, to 30 percent in 2007 during the Iraq War; after rising to 64 percent in 2009, it fell again, to 53 percent, in 2013 in the midst of National Security Agency (NSA) contractor Edward Snowden's revelations about U.S. spy programs.[32] The United States is held in lower

[30] Arjun Sreekumar, "Which Country Relies Most Heavily On Russian Gas?" *USA Today*, August 31, 2014.

[31] Matthew Karnitschnig, "German Businesses Urge Halt on Sanctions Against Russia," *Wall Street Journal*, May 1, 2014.

[32] Pew Research Center, *America's Global Image Remains More Positive than China's*, Pew Global Attitudes Project, July 18, 2013b, p. 10.

esteem in Germany than in any other European country polled except Greece and Russia. Recent revelations that German intelligence supported NSA data collection in Europe have yet to be neutralized.[33]

- Finally, there seems to be no real penalty for German free-riding.[34]

There are, however, important signs of a new, more security-oriented German attitude in response to Russia's activities in Ukraine. Slowly, Germany has exhibited a willingness to implement tougher economic and arms-transfer sanctions against Russia and has agreed that it would do more if necessary.[35] Chancellor Merkel has demonstrated strong leadership on the issue of sanctions against Russia and has helped shape a more realistic and tough-minded approach toward Russia. In mid-September, Germany urged reluctant European nations to implement a new round of tough sanctions aimed at increasing pressure on the Russian energy, defense, and financial sectors. Without Merkel's strong leadership, the sanctions imposed by the EU would have been much weaker.

Germany will become a NATO framework nation and lead multinational efforts designed to deliver defense capabilities more effectively. At the Wales NATO Summit, Germany agreed to compromise language that set 2 percent of GDP as a long-term defense spending target (though Berlin has no intention of reaching that target any time soon). In February 2015, Chancellor Merkel, together with French President François Hollande, negotiated the Minsk II ceasefire agree-

---

[33] One commentator concluded that an informal "no spying" agreement is needed to defuse this issue. See Robert Gerald Livingston, "Spies Get Between Germany and the United States," blog post, American Institute for Contemporary German Studies at Johns Hopkins University, July 15, 2014. Also see Greg Jaffe, "Germany's Merkel Will Be Key to Obama's Success at G-7," *Washington Post*, June 8, 2015.

[34] The author is grateful to RAND senior fellow David Gompert for his contributions to this discussion. Gompert believes that the United States should continue to pressure Germany to do more.

[35] Andrea Thomas, "Merkel Stresses Need to Prepare More Sanctions Against Russia," *Wall Street Journal*, September 1, 2014.

ment between Ukraine, Russia, and separatist leaders. Germany has also led Europe's response to the 2015 migrant crisis.

However, important differences of approach remain between many in Washington and Berlin on such issues as providing lethal arms to the Ukraine. Germany argues that "there is no military solution to the Ukrainian crisis." However, Putin continues to demonstrate that military power plays an important role in influencing the crisis. This major difference of approach aside, the United States should continue to press Germany to act as the empowered strategic leader that it could be.

Turkey: Whereas Germany's future directions will affect NATO capabilities in Eastern Europe, Turkey will affect NATO's view to the south. In the past few years, Turkey's bid for membership in the EU has stalled and lost important momentum. At the same time, Turkey's internal evolution—particularly the Justice and Development Party (abbreviated AKP in Turkish) government's crackdown on press freedoms and the heavy-handed use of force against the Gezi Park protests in May 2013—has tarnished Turkey's democratic credentials. European concerns have been reinforced by the lack of serious progress on the Kurdish issue and evidence of widespread corruption in the upper ranks of the AKP. Indeed, in many domestic policy areas Turkey has seemed to be moving in the wrong direction over the past few years.

In the June 2015 elections, President Recep Tayyip Erdogan's AKP lost its parliamentary election for the first time in more than a decade, partially because Erdogan had indicated his desire to change the constitution and enhance the power of the president. The AKP lost ground to the pro-Kurdish People's Democratic Party (HDP) and Erdogan was unable to form a coalition government. Instead, he lashed out against the Kurds and called snap elections. Tensions increased as a result of Erdogan's maneuvers and the tragic bombing of Kurdish peace activists in Ankara, but he won the November 2015 elections nonetheless and will move to strengthen his political control.

On the foreign policy front, Erdogan's intense and personal battle to force Assad's ouster has strained relations with Turkey's Western allies, especially the United States, which regards the struggle against ISIS as the top strategic priority. The United States and the majority of

Turkey's Western allies have criticized Turkey for not patrolling its borders adequately to prevent ISIS recruits from joining the fight. However, in recent months, Ankara and Washington have taken steps to narrow their differences and to coordinate policies. Under intense pressure from its NATO allies, Turkey allowed Kurdish fighters to transit its territory to help defend the Kurdish city of Kobane and it agreed to allow American aircraft to operate against ISIS from Turkish soil.

Turkey has the second-largest military in NATO. However, it is primarily a conscript army. Under the Kemalists, the army was largely seen as a mechanism for socializing Turkish youth and imbuing them with Kemalist ideals. The military acted as a state within a state and played a strong role in Turkish domestic politics, intervening when it felt secularism and democracy were endangered.

Under the AKP, which has strong Islamic roots, civilian control of the military has been strengthened and the threat of military intervention in domestic politics has significantly receded. The army is becoming smaller but more focused on a full range of NATO missions. The air force is well equipped with F-16s, airborne early warning aircraft, tankers, and transport aircraft. The navy is more of a coast guard, with a variety of smaller craft.[36] Therefore, Turkey has the capability to contribute significantly to NATO crisis-management operations, when willing.

Can Venus Become Mars?

NATO has taken several steps to address the changing security environment, diminishing military capability, and flagging will. These are preliminary steps and much will depend on implementation, but a framework is in place.

NATO is a remarkable institution that has remade itself and reset its purpose on several occasions. Most recently, in 2010 it was able to do so again by developing a new Strategic Concept that articulated three core tasks that together addressed the key security concerns of

[36] IISS, *The Military Balance 2012*, London, March 7, 2012, p. 162.

all member states. While NATO has existed for 66 years, it still has an important role to play in managing regional and global security and should remain at the center of U.S. security policy. NATO's consensus-based decisionmaking process can be slow and frustrating, but it usually manages to bring European nations around to a firm decision. Increasingly, that process is being used flexibly, allowing coalitions of the willing to operate within the Alliance.

NATO has conducted many successful military operations in the past few years. Those include ISAF operations in Afghanistan, a training mission in Iraq, naval counterterrorism and counter-piracy missions, a humanitarian/regime-change mission in Libya, and Baltic air policing. It has also supported the French-led military operation in Mali.

At the 2014 Wales Summit, NATO responded to concerns from the Baltic states and Poland that NATO was not adequately prepared to respond to Russia's hybrid warfare tactics.[37] The summit reaffirmed that collective defense is NATO's principal task. Heads of state issued a RAP that included several major elements:

- Development of a more-responsive NATO Response Force with a small (about 4,000 troops) but "very highly ready" joint spearhead force, able to deploy on two days' notice to defend any ally under attack.
- Assignment of corps-level operational headquarters and new local units to enhance deterrence.

[37] The purpose of hybrid operations is to gain political advantage through intimidation and covert operations while maintaining plausible deniability. Hybrid operations include, among other things, inflammatory propaganda, operations to create unrest among populations, bribery, kidnapping, cyberattacks, energy cutoffs, snap exercises and deployments near borders, provocative over-flights, use of military personnel in unmarked uniforms, provision of military equipment to insurgencies, nuclear threats, and, ultimately, outright invasion. Russia has tended to use hybrid operations in four phases: (1) creating instability in a neighboring state using intense propaganda; (2) infiltrating that destabilized state using intelligence, covert, and paramilitary operatives; (3) intimidating the target state and its partners by mobilizing troops along its border, threatening escalation, and rattling its nuclear saber; and (4) invading part of the target state using ground forces and modern military equipment.

- Maintenance of a larger NATO forward presence in the Baltic states and Poland, to be provided on a continuous rotational basis. This presence would provide infrastructure, prepositioned material, and be a "receiving force" for the NATO Response Force and other NATO units, should that be required. Host nations would support these troops. Poland and the Baltic states are concerned that there was no pledge given for a "permanent" presence in Eastern Europe.[38]

NATO commanders are satisfied with the RAP, but they note that key implementation decisions remain to be put into force, including the size of the forward presence, amount of prepositioned equipment, size and degree of readiness of the NATO Response Force, and degree of operational authority for the Supreme Allied Commander in Europe in time of crisis. Baltic air policing will be continued and strengthened. NATO will seek to increase its strategic awareness and develop rapid decisionmaking procedures.

The Alliance has also sought to create mechanisms so that European countries can maximize their dwindling defense budgets. These mechanisms are based on two concepts: "smart defense" and the Connected Forces Initiative. Smart defense encourages nations to pool and share resources in purchasing defense equipment, but this concept has distinct limits. At best, it may lead to a rationalization of training, exercise, and logistics facilities. Hopes for major multinational European programs have fallen on hard times. The Connected Forces Initiative is designed to maintain military interoperability after forces withdraw from ISAF. A third, potentially more promising initiative is called the framework nation concept, under which large nations such as Germany and Britain would cooperate with smaller nations to fill gaps in their capabilities. Used properly and with assured access to those capa-

---

[38] The United States has a rotational U.S. Army presence in these countries. NATO has refrained from using the word "permanent," to avoid raising issues about the status of the 1997 NATO-Russia Founding Act. That Act set up the NATO-Russia Council and limited the permanent deployment of significant NATO military equipment in NATO's new member states.

bilities, this concept could address NATO's redundancy problem and shift greater defense responsibility to larger European countries.

NATO has taken other steps to adapt to the new security environment created by Russia's more assertive policy. At the Wales Summit, it pledged to reverse defense spending declines and affirmed national goals of spending at least 2 percent of GDP on defense within a decade.[39] Most of that increase would be used to fill gaps identified in NATO's defense capabilities by NATO defense planners. While Germany and several others refused to agree to a firm commitment to meet that decade-long goal, at least the target remains. The United States might consider asking all of its global allies to meet this goal. If they would agree, combined defense spending among all U.S. partners might increase by more than $150 billion annually.

Thus far, however, the response has been uneven. The European Leadership Network recently reported that defense spending in the UK, Germany, Canada, Italy, Hungary, and Bulgaria would decrease in 2015. Defense budgets in states directly bordering Russia, including Latvia, Lithuania, Norway, Poland, and Romania, will increase.[40]

NATO also reaffirmed its nuclear deterrent posture in the face of pressure from some allies to withdraw the few remaining elements of the United States' nuclear arsenal in Europe.

NATO has also sought to strengthen its relations with its partners.[41] At the Wales Summit, NATO launched a Partner Interoperability Initiative with 24 "platform" members. Five of those nations, who have made particularly significant contributions to the Alliance, were designated as "enhanced" partners that would share a deeper dia-

---

[39] Historically, European defense spending as a percentage of GDP has been much higher. For example, in 1985, France spent 3.8 percent of GDP on defense, the United Kingdom spent 5.1 percent, and Germany spent 2.9 percent—all roughly double their current rates of spending today. See Stockholm International Peace Research Institute, undated.

[40] See Denitsa Raynova and Ian Kearns, "Report: Six European Members of NATO Will Cut Defense Spending and Break Agreement Made at Wales Summit," *NATOSource* blog, The Atlantic Council, February 26, 2015.

[41] In NATO parlance, partners are non-member nations who have varying degrees of ties with the Alliance. NATO has more partners than members.

logue and practical cooperation.[42] In addition, for vulnerable partners, NATO created the Defense and Related Security Capacity Building Initiative.

It has become popular in Washington to disparage NATO and its sometimes frustrating mechanisms. But the Alliance is stronger than the sum of its parts and would need to be reinvented if lost. Additional reforms are needed and defense gaps must be filled. Europe needs to be able to conduct missions without the United States, at least for small joint operations. A clear division of labor and role specialization could create forces tailored for certain missions and further stretch available defense funds. Coalitions of the willing and lead-nation operations could be facilitated more easily within the Alliance. Finally, decision-making could be further streamlined. Nevertheless, the NATO alliance remains by far the United States' most important partnership tool.

Assessing the Historical "Free Rider" Problem

The burden sharing, or free rider, problem has been a hearty perennial for NATO. Table 5.2 shows the historical ratio between non-U.S. NATO spending and U.S. defense spending.

With a roughly comparable GDP, Europe has historically spent between 43 percent and 78 percent of the United States' spending on defense. Today, Europeans in NATO spend about one-half as much. The principal factor in determining this ratio is U.S. defense spending, which has fluctuated dramatically. The ratio was lowest in the early 1950s (when Germany was not a member), in 1970, and in 2010, reflecting U.S. spending on wars in Korea, Vietnam, and Iraq, respectively. The ratio reached its peak in 1980 and 2000, periods of U.S. defense austerity. The only period of significant real growth in European defense spending was during the 1970s; otherwise, European defense expenditure has been remarkably flat in real terms. The problem has been that European defense spending has not kept up with its growth in GDP. The major factors that contributed to the growth of

---

[42] These enhanced partners are Sweden, Finland, Georgia, Jordan, and Australia.

Table 5.2
Ratio of U.S. to non-U.S. NATO Defense Spending (in billions of constant 2011 U.S. dollars)

Year	Europe	United States	Ratio Europe/U.S.
1950	73.3	133.7	0.59
1955	146.1	339.0	0.43
1960	164.1	345.0	0.47
1965	197.1	370.0	0.53
1970	207.2	462.6	0.45
1975	247.5	369.4	0.67
1980	286.3	377.3	0.76
1985	312.5	540.0	0.58
1990	330.5	527.2	0.63
1995	285.1	411.7	0.69
2000	307.3	394.2	0.78
2005	324.5	580.0	0.56
2010	336.7	720.3	0.47
2013	309.7	618.7	0.50

SOURCE: Stockholm International Peace Research Institute, undated.

European defense spending in the 1970s included economic growth at about 3 percent (down from the previous decade), an increased threat from Soviet missiles, a decline in U.S. defense spending as it withdrew from Vietnam, and threats by the U.S. Congress to withdraw its troops from Europe. The combination seems to have stimulated European nations to spend more on defense. Some, but not all, of these factors are present today.

Historically, efforts to create incentives or to manage the burden-sharing problem have taken four different approaches. The first approach (1966 to the mid-1980s) was based on the threat of U.S. troop withdrawals. With a series of resolutions and amendments from

1966 to 1975, Senator Mike Mansfield sought to use the threat of U.S. troop withdrawals to force Europe to contribute more and to lessen U.S. costs.[43] As noted, that effort—plus other factors relating to economic growth and the Soviet threat—may have had a positive effect: European defense spending grew by 44 percent between 1970 and 1984.[44] But problems remained. In 1984, Senator Sam Nunn sought to force the allies to live up to a 1978 pledge to increase defense spending by 3 percent annually, to provide facilities for ten reinforcing U.S. divisions, and to acquire a 30-day supply of conventional munitions. His amendment would have withdrawn 90,000 troops from Europe by 1990 if those nations did not deliver on his demands. The amendment never passed the Senate.

Some suggest using the possibility of U.S. troop withdrawals today to stimulate European defense spending. Absent the new Russian challenges to Europe, that might work. But troop withdrawals now run the high risk of being misread in both Russia and Europe.

During the past few decades, a second approach has been tried. At the 1999 Washington Summit, the 2002 Prague Summit, and the 2010 Lisbon Summit, heads of state agreed to meet various defense capability goals. The first attempt created a laundry list of items that proved impossible to implement. By the time of the Lisbon Summit, the list had been pared down to ten critical items and some progress has been made to address those needs. Following up on this general approach, NATO's two supreme commanders now generate a critical capabilities shortfall list, and NATO's Defense Planning Process seeks to direct national expenditures to close those gaps. Despite these agreed capability goals, European defense spending as a percentage of GDP fell steadily during this period.

A third approach is reliance on percentage targets. During the Cold War, the United States sought to stimulate the growth in European defense spending by setting a 3 percent annual growth target.

---

[43] Peter Lazar, *The Mansfield Amendments and the U.S. Commitment in Europe, 1966–1975*, thesis, Monterey, Calif.: Naval Postgraduate School, June 2003.

[44] Robert Bowie, "Nunn Amendment: NATO Must Do More on Conventional Arms," *Christian Science Monitor*, June 29, 1984.

More recently, percentage targets have been suggested for deployable forces, for sustainable forces, for the proportion of capabilities supplied by any one country, for the relationship between defense spending and GDP, and for defense investment.

A fourth approach, initiated by former NATO Secretary General Anders Fogh Rasmussen, focused on what he called smart defense. This is an effort to have groups of nations purchase equipment collectively and share it when needed. Some progress has been made to create more-efficient ways to acquire military equipment, but the overall impact has not been dramatic.

Russian aggression in Ukraine has begun to shift attitudes about defense spending in Europe. To take full advantage of this shift, the following list of suggestions might now fall on fertile ground:

- *Pursue the 2-percent defense spending pledge.* One interim step for NATO is to create an incremental plan for achieving the 2-percent goal by 2025, as well as a scorecard to record progress. A related approach would be to assure that any spending increases are spent on NATO priority shortfall items. The United States' Asian partners should consider a similar pledge. The two key nations are Germany and Japan, which spend 1.3 percent and 1.0 percent, respectively. If these two nations could meet the 2-percent goal, the U.S. defense burden would be greatly relieved.
- *Set a goal for increased European military independence.* Europe needs to have a fuller spectrum of military capabilities. This is consistent with the current goal of having no single NATO country provide more than 50 percent of the capabilities needed for any one mission. That goal should be pressed. In addition, NATO's European members should be able to conduct three small joint operations (land, naval, and air) independently of the United States by 2020.
- *Encourage greater regional military cooperation among allies.* NATO has sought to encourage smart defense measures by having clusters of allies pool funds for defense acquisition and share those military assets once purchased. More recently, NATO has developed the next level of regional cooperation by having larger, framework

nations lead smaller nations—with regard to both defense acquisition and military operations. The efficiencies created by greater regional cooperation are an important element in empowering our partners.

- *Identify niche and specialty capabilities for allies and partners.* The United States should encourage smaller partners to develop niche capabilities that would prove particularly useful to U.S.-led coalition operations.
- *Create geographic and functional divisions of labor.* As the United States becomes more engaged in meeting challenges to partners from Russia and China, those partners need to offset that U.S. effort by contributing more to stabilization efforts in North Africa, the Middle East, and Southeast Asia.
- *Consult bilaterally on defense capabilities.* The Pentagon should consult more carefully with its principal military partners to get a clearer understanding as to what military contributions partners might make to coalition operations, given their defense spending plans. The Pentagon also needs to clarify the degree to which partners might count on U.S. military support for various sets of contingencies.
- *Strengthen military interoperability with NATO allies and partners.* In the post-ISAF environment, the United States should use NATO's Connected Forces Initiative and the NATO Response Force vigorously to maintain NATO military interoperability and should support efforts to strengthen the NATO Response Force. U.S. European Command should have enhanced interoperability with NATO allies as a principal mission.
- *Create new NATO multinational battalions in each of the Baltic states.* This could be accomplished by taking the one U.S. Army company currently deployed in each Baltic state and organizing it with a host-nation company and a company from other European nations. The headquarters might be commanded by a U.S. officer.
- *Create new resilience support teams in each of the Baltic states.* These teams could be loosely modeled on the provincial reconstruction teams used by ISAF in Afghanistan. They would use a mix of

civilian and military assets to reduce the risks posed by Russian hybrid operations to front-line nations.

- *Use and expand the new NATO enhanced partnership mechanism.* The Wales Summit created five "enhanced opportunity partners" (Finland, Sweden, Georgia, Jordan, and Australia). Separate memoranda of understanding have been signed by NATO with Finland and Sweden. The five enhanced partners will have to move on separate tracks so that none are retarded by progress with the others. Finland and Sweden should be encouraged to join the Alliance as soon as their publics approve. Japan and South Korea should become NATO enhanced opportunity partners so that all of the "Article 5 partners" share maximum political consultations and military interoperability.
- *Focus on NATO air power.* Europe has adequate fighter aircraft for now, but attrition will affect that calculation over the next decade. In addition, Europe has major gaps in enabling areas such as strategic lift; air-to-air refueling; and intelligence, surveillance, and reconnaissance. Airpower is increasingly the military instrument of choice, but European contributions to enablers is inadequate today and its fighter aircraft contributions may be inadequate a decade from now. A major NATO review of European airpower is required.
- *Strengthen existing NATO institutions for maximum unity and rapid response.* For NATO, this would include greater intelligence sharing and common situational awareness, planning for contingencies in the northeast, understanding the nature of hybrid threats, making forces more responsive for emergency use, and streamlining decisionmaking in times of crisis.
- *Discuss impact of U.S. defense cuts.* U.S. defense cuts and the Quadrennial Defense Review "win, deny" strategy may have a significant impact on the U.S. ability to rapidly deploy forces to Europe should the United States be engaged in a major military operation in Asia or the Middle East. This may shift the concept of burden-sharing from a political to a military one.
- *Work more closely with NATO on the so-called Third Offset and Air-Sea Battle.* NATO's Allied Command Transformation, in partic-

ular, is keen to learn more about these new U.S. concepts and what they mean for the Alliance.

Transatlantic Trade and Security

Transatlantic trade accounts for $5 trillion in annual sales, while transatlantic investment is measured at about $2.7 trillion annually. Transatlantic partners are each other's largest trade and investment partners. Together, they account for about 46 percent of global GDP.[45] This critical economic bond reinforces political and military ties, but freer trade could do more. A study by the Centre for Economic Policy Research found that by further reducing or eliminating tariffs, non-tariff barriers, and excessive regulations, the European economy would grow by about $135 billion annually and the U.S. economy would grow by about $107 billion annually.[46]

In July 2013, the United States and the European Union began negotiating on a new round of trade agreements called TTIP (Transatlantic Trade and Investment Partnership). It is hoped that the freer trade prompted by such an accord would help to stimulate economies still emerging from the 2008 recession. The main areas of negotiation are market access, including tariff elimination, regulatory issues, and non-tariff barriers, and rulemaking in areas such as intellectual property.[47] The Republican-led Congress and President Obama have passed fast-track legislation, which should stimulate a final round of negotiations with both Asia and the EU.

TTIP is more than an emerging trade agreement—it is a way to strengthen the transatlantic bond. It reinforces the importance of global rules for a liberal trading order and, if used properly, can serve as a magnet to attract emerging economies to that same liberal order. TTIP could become an important tool for Western nations to use to

---

[45] Binnendijk, 2014a, p. 286.

[46] European Commission, *Transatlantic Trade and Investment Partnership: The Economic Analysis Explained*, September 2013.

[47] Binnendijk, 2014a, p. 286.

deal with the various alternative governance models being served up by potential adversaries.[48] U.S. negotiators hope to complete Trans-Pacific Partnership (TPP) talks first, since they are more mature.

Europe in North Africa, the Middle East, and Asia

One of the conclusions of Chapters Three and Four of this report is that the United States is in danger of being overstretched, with extended commitments to partners, a declining defense budget, declining desire to engage in long-term stability operations, and increasingly complex challenges, including those posed by potential adversaries. It was noted that the Defense Department's new defense strategy of "win, deny" and the broader pivot to Asia create additional responsibilities, especially for NATO. Europe's responsibilities need to grow in North Africa, the Middle East, and even in Asia.

The United States and its European partners have been cooperating closely in North Africa. The NATO Libya operation marked a turning point for two reasons. First, the United States let its European allies take a greater leadership role, with European aircraft dropping a large majority of the munitions on Gaddafi's forces. The United States conducted some air strikes but generally provided enablers and resupplied munitions stockpiles. Second, NATO did not follow the regime change operation with a credible stability operation, with disastrous consequences for Libya. Subsequently, the United States has supported French-led operations in Niger. France now has 3,000 troops permanently deployed in Mali, Chad, Niger, and Burkina Faso, primarily to deal with Boko Haram. The United States, through U.S. Africa Command, is also expanding its presence there in cooperation with France to support counterterrorism missions and drone flights.[49] Europe is no stranger to North Africa: From 2004 to 2013, the EU conducted

---

[48] Daniel S. Hamilton and Pedro Schwartz, *A Transatlantic Free Trade Area—A Boost to Economic Growth?* Brussels: New Direction, undated.

[49] Craig Whitlock, "Pentagon Expands Footprint in Africa," *Washington Post*, September 2, 2014.

at least 13 separate operations in ten African nations.[50] Having the United States play a supporting role may in fact be a useful model for future forward partnering operations in that region.

Europe has taken the lead in North Africa, with the United States supporting those efforts, but the reverse has been true in the Middle East. U.S. regime change and stabilization operations in Iraq nearly divided the Alliance. In Afghanistan, however, every NATO country had some involvement and, generally, one European soldier served for every two Americans. Combat operations have shifted to Afghan forces, but some European troops will join their American counterparts in continuing training and counterterrorism operations until the end of 2016. ISAF fatigue, however, contributed to a combined reluctance to engage in the Syrian civil war. At some point, that war will end and NATO is likely to be asked to conduct reconstruction operations there.

More immediately, European nations are key to the coalition to "degrade and ultimately destroy" ISIS. Thirteen members of the NATO alliance have joined the United States to provide either direct military support or military assistance. Another 12 provided economic or political support.[51] The Alliance itself, however, is not a party to the counter-ISIS coalition.

Europe also had fundamental interests in Asia, including trade and security issues. EU-Asian trade has increased four-fold in the past decade—reaching $1.1 trillion in 2012.[52] Any major military confrontation in Asia affecting the United States would have a profound impact on Europe, including the possibility of triggering an Article 5 commitment.

---

[50] Charles Barry and Samuel Greene, "European Military Capabilities in the 21st Century," National Defense University working draft, January 2013, p. 159. The EU missions were in the following countries: Congo, Sudan, South Sudan, Egypt, Chad, Guinea-Bissau, Somalia, Uganda, Horn of Africa, and Mali.

[51] Sebastian Payne, "What the 60-Plus Members of the Anti-Islamic State Coalition Are Doing," *Washington Post*, September 25, 2014.

[52] Binnendijk, 2014a, p. 276.

However, Europe has no coherent strategic approach to Asia.[53] It could play a much larger constructive role in coordination with the United States, and a consultative mechanism needs to be established. Trade agreements are a first important step. The EU has completed trade negotiations with South Korea and is conducting bilateral talks with India, Japan, Malaysia, Singapore, Thailand, and Vietnam. Eventually, TTIP will need to be harmonized with these bilateral efforts and the U.S.-Asian TPP. The purpose would be not only freer trade and harmonization, but to bring China into what would amount to a modern, rules-based trilateral U.S.-EU-Asian set of relationships.

While Europe is unlikely to contribute significantly to security operations in Asia given pressing business on its own borders, there are ways in which NATO can engage in Asian security. It needs to create closer partnerships with Japan, Australia, and South Korea, which also have collective security commitments from the United States. Six European nations participated in the most recent U.S.-led RIMPAC (Rim of the Pacific) exercise, and that effort can grow. In September 2014, Japan and NATO conducted their first ever joint naval exercise in the Gulf of Aden.[54]

Other defense cooperation might include

- creating a NATO-ASEAN forum for periodic consultations
- establishing NATO liaison offices in key Asian capitals
- organizing a special Asian office in the NATO International Staff
- conducting exercises for humanitarian assistance training
- holding annual nuclear planning meetings for all nations covered by the U.S. umbrella
- developing closer cooperation on ballistic missile defense
- participating in occasional joint naval patrols in the Pacific
- encouraging Japan and South Korea to conduct joint operations together
- facilitating Asian participation in the NATO Response Force

---

[53] Binnendijk, 2014a, p. 77.

[54] NATO, "NATO and Japan Conduct First Ever Joint Counter-Piracy Drill," web page, October 3, 2014b.

- developing common approaches to cyber defense
- coordinating on special operations forces counterterrorism operations
- expanding efforts on the role of the military in democracies.[55]

China might be invited into some of these initiatives, to make clear that this is not an effort to contain China.

Perhaps the most important contribution that Europe can make to Asian security is to highlight the role of institutions, norms, and the rule of law in conflict resolution. EU institutions and procedures have helped to reconcile neighbors who spent centuries fighting each other. That degree of reconciliation and norm-setting has not taken place in Asia. A good place to start would be with maritime disputes, where Europeans have worked out compromises that have avoided conflict.

A Regional Strategy for Europe

The most difficult European security problem is providing adequate support, reassurance, and deterrence to vulnerable nations that lie between NATO and Russia. Europe's declining capability and will to wield power has been based on the failing post–Cold War paradigm. Most European nations are still underperforming; European military units will be more modern but smaller and less sustainable. France and the United Kingdom remain the two most capable and willing allies, but even that may be eroding due to continued defense budget cuts, heavy French deployments, and continuing aspirations for independence in Scotland.

Europe's disengagement may be slowly changing in response to Russian behavior. Accelerating and sustaining that change needs to be a top U.S. priority. Germany holds the key to reversing European capabilities and will; it seems to have turned a corner in the right direction,

---

[55] From Hans Binnendijk, "The American Pivot and NATO Engagement in the Indo-Pacific Basin," Center for Transatlantic Relations, May 2014b. Also see Franklin D. Kramer, *NATO Global Partners: Strategic Opportunities and Imperatives in a Globalized World*, Washington, D.C.: Atlantic Council, March 2013; and Binnendijk, 2014a, pp. 199–216.

but its emergence will be slow. NATO as an institution has created a degree of strategic unity among transatlantic partners that should not be underestimated—but continued long-term adaptation will be necessary. A new transatlantic division of global labor is emerging and needs to be reinforced, which may help both sides of the Atlantic cope with ever-growing global challenges.

The United States' regional strategy for Europe is clear. It is to maximize Alliance unity in the face of new provocations from Putin's Russia, to deter Russia from attacking NATO members, and to prevent Russia from annexing more of Ukraine. It is using diplomatic instruments for the first element, military instruments for the second, and coercive instruments for the third. Though Europe is divided on many issues, the Wales NATO Summit showed a new level of resolve with regard to common defense. Also, the EU has shown new cohesion in declaring sometimes painful economic sanctions against Russia's annexation of Crimea and incursions into the Donbas area of Ukraine.

At the same time, NATO cannot neglect the new challenges facing it to the south. Instability in North Africa and in Syria has led to massive immigration flows that have now brought hundreds of thousands of refugees to northern Europe. NATO forces may well be engaged in operations to manage that flow of refugees and eventually to provide stabilization operations in these areas.

Given these challenges, there is little room for U.S. retrenchment in Europe. Nor should the United States be so assertive that it breaks unity with major European powers. The United States is overextended and needs its European allies to play a stronger global role. While not perfectly suited, a more collaborative approach may best fit the European situation.

There is potential tension between the need to keep a reassuring U.S. military presence in Europe and the need for European nations to share more of the defense burden. To the extent that the United States reassures, Europe has the opportunity to free-ride. That tension cannot be solved by U.S. troop withdrawals, as some advocate. As discussed previously, greater burden-sharing will need to be stimulated in other ways. Europe is beginning to understand that defense burden imbalance needs to be corrected, but continued U.S. pressure will be required. Europe is awakening to the challenge posed by Putin, but Europe cannot return to a sole focus on common defense and disregard its crisis-management responsibilities in the Middle East. Europe also needs to play a more active role in Asia. The policy challenge for the United States is how to encourage its European partners to seize this larger role without appearing to be weakening the U.S. commitment to European defense at the same time.

CHAPTER SIX

Asian Partners and Inadequate Security Structures

The U.S. Pivot to Asia

The United States' 2012 policy to rebalance to Asia was initially called the "pivot" to Asia, which created the impression that the United States was pivoting away from other partners.[1] The intent was to rebalance strategic attention and some defense resources to the Asian theater, so the Obama administration began calling it a "rebalance." Instead, however, "pivot" has stuck internationally.[2] The pivot was based on three core assumptions. First, Asia would be the most important center of both opportunity and risk. Second, Europe would be stable and secure. Third, the Arab Spring would allow the United States to avoid engaging in more major ground wars in the Middle East. The second and third assumptions are now questionable, but the first remains and is seen by the Obama administration as sufficient grounds to sustain its pivot policy.[3]

The National Intelligence Council's *Global Trends 2030* report concluded that by 2030 Asia would surpass both North America and Europe combined, in terms of global power, based on a combination

---

[1] For a more-detailed description of the pivot strategy, see Chapters Two and Three of Binnendijk, 2014a.

[2] Also see Jeffrey A. Bader, *Obama and China's Rise: An Insider's Account of America's Asia Strategy*, Washington, D.C.: Brookings Institution, 2012.

[3] For a good discussion of this strategy, see Phillip C. Saunders, *The Rebalance to Asia: U.S.-China Relations and Regional Security*, Washington, D.C.: National Defense University, Strategic Forum No. 281, August 2013.

of GDP, population, defense spending, and investment in technology.[4] Whether that prediction is borne out or not, Asia is on the rise. U.S. trade with Asia in 2012 was $1.1 trillion dollars, or about one-third of total U.S. trade.[5] Asian sea lanes are already the busiest in the world. All of this provides an opportunity for Asian nations to continue to enjoy economic success and raise their people from poverty. At the same time, it provides opportunities for lucrative American trade and investment.

The notion of a strategic pivot to Asia emerged in a 2011 *Foreign Policy* article by then–Secretary of State Hillary Clinton that called for greater U.S. investments in Asia to "sustain our leadership and advance our values."[6] The Department of Defense's January 2012 Defense Strategic Guidance picked up the theme and pledged to shift the U.S. force structure toward Asia.[7] The United States will now have 60 percent of its naval and air assets focused on Asia and will deploy Marines forward in Australia.

The pivot policy was soon misinterpreted: China saw it as further containment; Europe saw it as abandonment; most saw it as primarily a military policy; many saw it as primarily rhetorical. These "myths" were rebutted, but misunderstanding continues.[8]

Strategic Dangers in Asia

The U.S. pivot to Asia was based not only on opportunity, but on the need to manage a region that has only become more dangerous since 2011. *The Military Balance 2014* begins its assessment of Asia by saying "Across Asia, continuing efforts to strengthen military capabilities have

---

4 U.S. National Intelligence Council, 2012, p. 16.

5 Binnendijk, 2014a, p. 274.

6 Hillary Rodham Clinton, "America's Pacific Century," *Foreign Policy*, October 11, 2011.

7 U.S. Department of Defense, *Sustaining U.S. Global Leadership: Priorities for 21st Century Defense*, Washington, D.C., January 2012, p. 2.

8 For example, see Binnendijk, 2014a, pp. 29–48.

taken place against rising strategic tensions among major powers . . ."[9] The greatest risk of U.S. involvement in major-power conflict lies in Asia. The geopolitical landscape evokes comparisons with the 19th century, when power was used to gain territory, nationalism drove policy, and international norms and institutions were limited. This cocktail of dangerous ingredients includes

- a rising potential peer competitor (China) that feels history has disadvantaged it while it was weak and is now determined to shape a new status quo, possibly at the expense of U.S. partners
- a new nuclear rogue state (North Korea) with mercurial leadership that increasingly threatens South Korea, Japan, and the United States
- technology that is making China and North Korea increasingly dangerous over time, as Beijing builds its A2/AD capability and Pyongyang develops both more-accurate, longer-range missiles and nuclear warhead miniaturization capabilities
- U.S. partners in Japan and South Korea that are both alarmed at what they see as provocations from China and North Korea, respectively, and that appear willing to respond more firmly to future provocations
- the rise in defense spending in Asia by 23 percent since 2010 to $321 billion in 2013, creating what some have called an arms race[10]
- rising nationalism in most Asian countries, especially in China and Japan
- minimal reconciliation along the lines of what occurred in Europe
- multiple flashpoints in the East and South China seas, on the Korean Peninsula, and in Taiwan
- weak rules and procedures for settling contending claims
- inadequate U.S. influence over the policies of its partners
- weak regional security institutions

---

[9] IISS, 2014, p. 201.

[10] IISS, 2014, p. 204.

- a hub-and-spoke set of defensive alliances between the United States and its five treaty allies (Japan, South Korea, Australia, Philippines, and Thailand) with inadequate defense cooperation among U.S. allies.

The next few sections will explore the major areas of tension and nations that are potentially vulnerable as a result, the nature of the current security architecture in Asia, U.S. military considerations, three key U.S. partners, the potential role of free trade agreements, and a possible approach to managing China.

Areas of Tension and Vulnerable Nations

There are at least six potential scenarios for major power conflict in East Asia. Four focus on China while two start with North Korea but also involve China. As a result, most U.S. partners in the region can be considered to be at some risk.[11]

The first scenario is a clash between China and a U.S. partner with contending claims in the South China Sea—Vietnam would be most likely. China's claims in the South China Sea are extreme, and Vietnam contests them vigorously. Since Vietnam is not a U.S. treaty ally, China may be more inclined to test Vietnam through force in the Spratly Islands, as it did in the Paracels. Incidents between Chinese and Vietnamese ships are frequent. China's efforts to create islands out of seven reefs, including Fiery Cross Reef, Subi Reef, and Mischief Reef, and to build airstrips capable of handling jet fighters have heightened the tension significantly. The map in Figure 6.1 highlights the contending claims.

In this scenario, a hypothetical incident could escalate at sea, but probably not to a major land war. While the United States would chasten China should it initiate escalation, the United States would be unlikely to become involved directly since it has no binding security commitments with Vietnam; however, the United States might provide military

[11] See Gompert, Binnendijk, and Lin, 2014, pp. 217–246.

Figure 6.1
Disputed Regions in the South China Sea

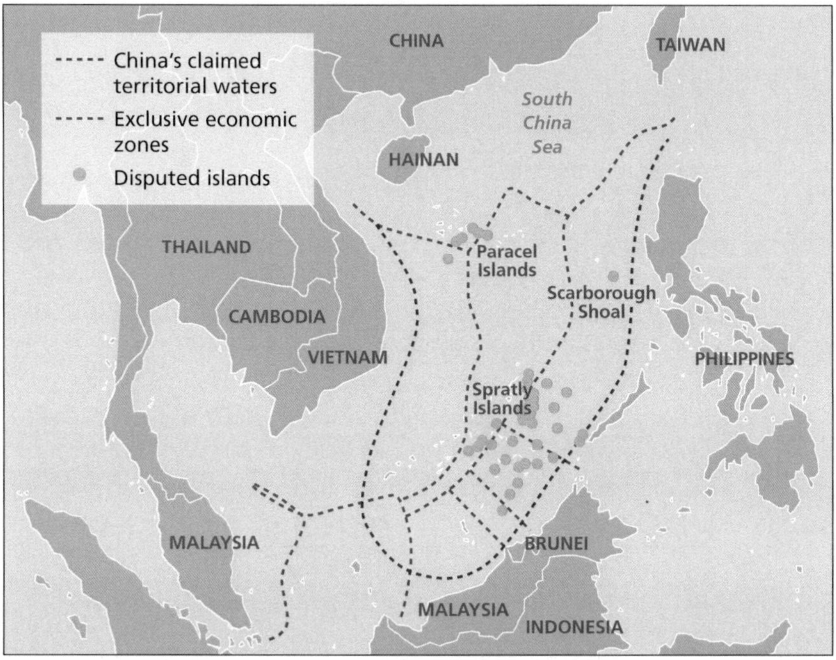

RAND *RR1210-6.1*

assistance to Vietnam. In another case, the United States does have a security treaty with the Philippines. That treaty is unlikely to be triggered over the disputed Scarborough Shoal, but it might come into play over the Second Thomas Shoal, where the Philippines have deployed a few marines on a grounded World War II–era tank landing ship.

The second scenario involves a China-Japan confrontation over the Senkaku/Diaoyu Islands. Japan claimed sovereignty in 1895, and China did not seriously contest this claim until 1971, after mineral resources were discovered in the region. China's claim dates from 1534 and rests on the case that the islands should have reverted to Chinese control—along with Taiwan—under the Potsdam Declaration and the San Francisco Treaty. The United States administered the islands as part of Okinawa and turned administrative control over to Japan in

1972. Now China is pressing its claims and declared an air defense identification zone in 2013 that overlaps with those of Japan, Taiwan, and South Korea (see Figure 6.2).[12]

This confrontation poses a higher risk for the United States, given the near-daily frequency of incidents around the islands, growing nationalism, lack of reconciliation between the contestants, and U.S.

Figure 6.2
East China Sea Air Defense Identification Zone

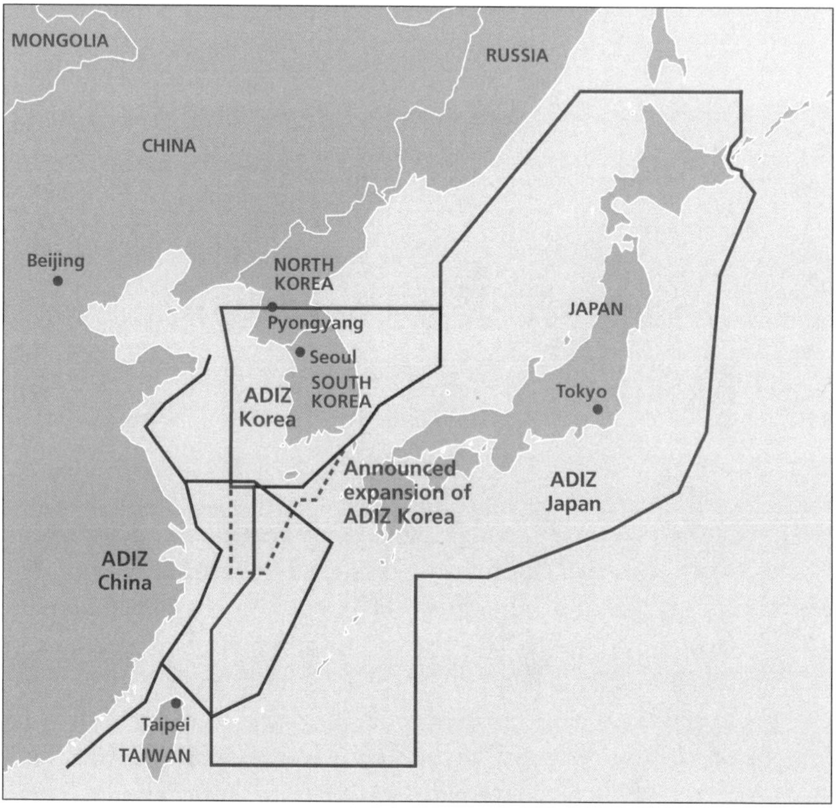

NOTE: ADIZ = air defense identification zone.
RAND *RR1210-6.2*

---

[12] See Michael D. Swaine, "Chinese Views and Commentary on the East China Sea Air Defense Identification Zone (ECS ADIZ)," *China Leadership Monitor*, No. 43, Spring 2014.

recognition of Japan's administrative control of the islands. The United States takes no position on the legal claims but insists on a peaceful solution. The United States has also stated that its security treaty with Japan extends to Japanese administration of the Senkakus. It is not clear what degree of escalation would trigger a U.S. military response.

Scenario three involves Taiwan. The dangerous cross-strait tensions of the Chen Shui-Bian period appear to be over for now. Cultural ties are flourishing and China is now Taiwan's largest trading partner. The 2010 Economic Cooperation Framework Agreement and two follow-up agreements could set the basis for even greater economic ties, but those agreements are opposed in Taiwan by the nationalist opposition. Chinese efforts to constrain democratic processes in Hong Kong do not bode well for long-term political integration. Another reason for concern is how China might handle things if the opposition Democratic Progressive Party candidate wins Taiwan's next presidential election in January 2016.

At the same time, defense of Taiwan will become increasingly more problematic over the next decade, as Chinese military capabilities advance. Taiwan's 2013 National Defense Report concluded that, by 2020, China could be in a position to invade and occupy Taiwan.[13] China's patience may erode as its capability mounts, especially if January 2016 elections bring the Democratic Progressive Party to power. The United States continues to provide defensive weapons to Taiwan, much to the consternation of Beijing. The U.S. obligation to defend Taiwan rests on imprecise language in the Taiwan Relations Act, rather than on a binding mutual defense treaty.[14]

The fourth scenario involves direct confrontation between the United States and China over freedom of the seas and airways. The 2001 Hainan Island incident is a case in point. China continues to harass U.S. intelligence-gathering flights well beyond the 12-mile territorial sea zone. In August 2014, China conducted a dangerous intercept of an American P-8 Poseidon and, more recently, issued urgent

---

[13] As cited in IISS, 2014, p. 201.

[14] Section 2 of the 1979 Taiwan Relations Act states that "any effort to determine the future of Taiwan by other than peaceful means . . . (is) of grave concern to the United States."

warnings as a P-8 flew a mission over contested waters in the South China Sea.[15] Alternative intelligence-gathering means are available, but the United States is unwilling to cede its international rights. U.S. National Security Advisor Susan Rice recently visited Beijing in part to manage these dangerous incidents. Some suggest an arrangement under which the number of U.S. intelligence flights might be reduced in exchange for Chinese acceptance of the remaining flights.

Scenario five involves escalation of an incident between North and South Korea. The analogy is the events of 2010, this time with escalation. In March of that year, a North Korean torpedo sank the ROK corvette *Cheonan*. In November, North Korea bombarded Yeonpyeong Island as part of a broader DPRK challenge to the UN Northern Limit Line (depicted in Figure 6.3).

Seoul showed considerable restraint in 2010, but the Park government—like its predecessor—has promised to respond more assertively the next time. The United States still remains in operational command of UN forces in Korea and, for now, has mechanisms to moderate Seoul's response. A modification of this North Korean scenario might envision Pyongyang firing missiles near Japan or U.S. forces in Asia and triggering a reaction that escalates.

The final scenario, the implosion of the Pyongyang government, may be the most dangerous. A North Korean collapse has been widely predicted for decades, yet the grandson of Kim Il-sung, the Great Leader, remains in power. North Korea has lost much of its industrial and agricultural base and has great difficulty meeting the basic needs of its people. It uses further repression to compensate. A collapse could involve civil war and a lashing out at South Korea and Japan. Managing this scenario would require close consultation with Beijing on issues relating to the collapse, the conduct of war, control of nuclear weapons, refugees, and degree of U.S. participation. China is unwilling to consult closely on these issues for fear that the consultations themselves would further weaken the Pyongyang government. The United States will need to find a channel to discuss this contingency with Beijing.

---

[15] Jim Sciutto, "Exclusive: China Warns U.S. Surveillance Plane," *CNN.com*, May 26, 2015.

Figure 6.3
ROK-DPRK Maritime Boundaries

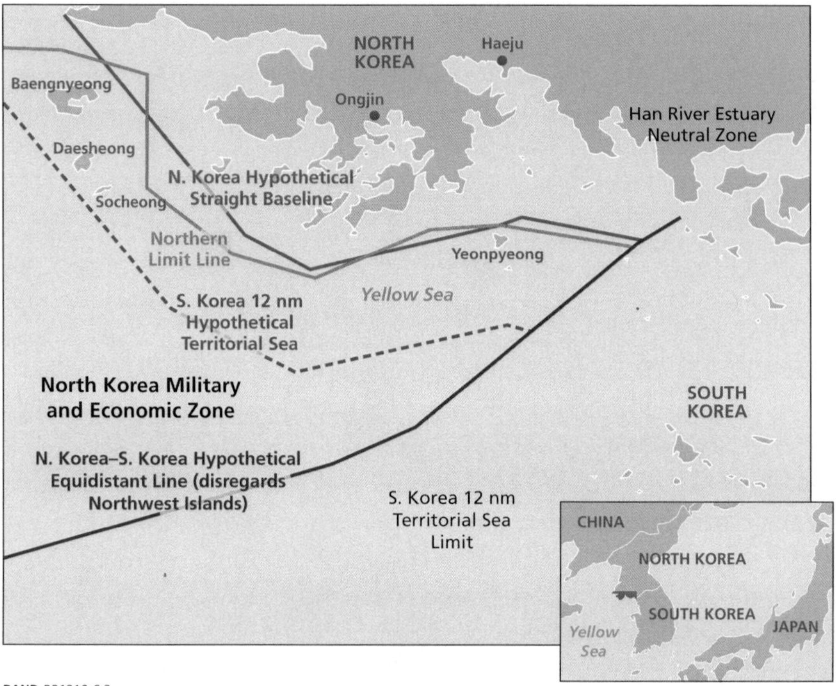

RAND *RR1210-6.3*

Asia's Security Architecture Is Underdeveloped

Asia has underdeveloped institutions to handle such contingencies. While economic integration in Asia is moving apace, security architectures lag far behind. The most prominent international institution in Asia is ASEAN, established in 1967 and chartered in 2008–2009. It promotes the "ASEAN Way," which emphasizes respect for sovereignty, non-interference in domestic affairs, and a pragmatic approach to manage tensions. Its main purpose is to be a neutral forum for its dialogue partners. It had some early successes in managing differences between four of its founding states and worked more closely with the United States after the end of the Vietnam War.[16]

---

[16] Binnendijk, 2014a, p. 113–116.

ASEAN has spread its diplomatic reach by creating ASEAN+3 (with China, Japan, and South Korea) and later the East Asian Summit. The ASEAN Regional Forum (ARF) was created in 1994 to hold annual discussions among foreign ministers on security issues. North Korea is represented in the ARF. Later, the ASEAN Defense Ministers' Meeting Plus was established for defense ministers to meet; humanitarian assistance exercises have been held under its auspices. The United States has sought to strengthen its ties to ASEAN, and now President Obama regularly attends the East Asian Summit. However, ASEAN is a modest organization with an annual budget of about $16 million. None of these arrangements provides hard security for ASEAN's members.

The United States has defense treaties with Japan, South Korea, Australia, the Philippines, and Thailand. These are hub-and-spoke arrangements with good cooperation between Japan and Australia, but limited cooperation between the two most important partners: Japan and South Korea. Beyond U.S. commitments, there is also a series of bilateral arrangements that together make up the Five-Power Defense Agreements—which includes the United Kingdom, Australia, New Zealand, Malaysia, and Singapore—but this is focused primarily on Malaysia and Singapore.

As maritime controversies have intensified, Japan, South Korea, Australia, and the Philippines have all sought ways to strengthen their security ties to the United States. For example, defense guidelines with Japan are being revised, command and control arrangements with South Korea are being modified, and the Philippines is giving the United States greater access to military installations. Vietnam has also moved to improve ties with the United States, such as offering occasional access to Cam Ranh Bay. The United States has partially lifted the prohibition on the sale of lethal military equipment to Vietnam, especially for maritime purposes. However, all of these countries also have critical trade relationships with China and seek ways to enhance their security without endangering their economic progress. Table 6.1 summarizes U.S. defense relationships with selected Asian partners.

This security structure and level of defense spending are inadequate for any of these nations to confront China in a major military operation without massive U.S. involvement. The selected countries in Table 6.1 together spend less on defense than what China spends alone. Only Japan, South Korea, Australia, and (to some degree) Singapore have modern forces capable of projecting power. The degree of military interoperability among these countries has been minimal. To correct this, Japan has sought to develop closer defense ties with Australia, the Philippines, and Vietnam.[17] Nonetheless, regional mechanisms are weak and have no ability to deter China. There are no collective defense pacts outside of those created by the United States and the United Kingdom. So unlike Europe and its NATO alliance, the burden currently falls squarely on the United States and its three capable bilateral allies. A NATO-like organization is unlikely to form in Asia, but the United States will need to insist on greater multilateral security cooperation among its bilateral allies to share this burden.

Two Pivotal Partners: Japan and India

The future directions taken by Japan and India will have a profound impact on the United States' posture in Asia.

Japan:[18] Japan is the United States' most powerful partner in Asia, yet—for historical reasons—has consistently under-contributed to the security of East Asia. Japan has the world's third largest economy, runs a current account surplus, has begun to stimulate its economy out of decade-long stagnation, has low inflation, and has unemployment levels that are one-half that of the United States. It has limited itself to spending less than 1 percent of its GDP on defense—it will spend about $53 billion on defense in 2015. Per capita, that is about one-quarter of what the United States spends, about one-half of the NATO 2-percent goal, and less than one-third of what China spends on defense.

[17] For more details on growing cooperation, see Patrick M. Cronin, Richard Fontaine, Zachary M. Hosford, Oriana Skylar Mastro, Ely Ratner, and Alexander Sullivan, *The Emerging Power Web: The Rise of Bilateral Intra-Asian Security Ties*, Center for a New American Security, June 2013.

[18] The author is grateful for the contributions to this section made by David Gompert.

Table 6.1
U.S. Defense Relationships with Selected Asian Partners

Country	U.S. Commitment	2013 Defense Budget/Active Force	U.S. Forces	U.S. Military Cooperation
Japan	1960 Treaty of Mutual Cooperation and Security to "meet the common danger"	\$59 billion/247,000	48,000 troops	high degree
Republic of Korea	1953 Mutual Defense Treaty to "meet common danger"	\$32 billion/655,000 (4.5 million reserves)	25,000 troops	high degree
Australia	1951 ANZUS Treaty (originally included New Zealand but now bilateral) to "meet common danger"	\$26 billion/56,000	2,500 troops	high degree
Philippines	1951 Mutual Defense Treaty to "meet common danger" (does not apply to Scarborough Shoal)	\$2.2 billion/125,000	access but no bases	2014 Enhanced Defense Cooperation Agreement
Thailand	1954 Manila Pact to "meet common danger"	\$6.2 billion/360,000	possible joint airfield use	U.S. military assistance
Taiwan	1979 Taiwan Relations Act to meet threats of "grave concern"	\$10.3 billion/290,000	none	average U.S. arms sales of \$1 billion
Indonesia	none	\$8.3 billion/395,500	possible use of airfields	2010 Defense Framework Agreement
Vietnam	none	\$3.8 billion/482,000	visits to Cam Ranh Bay	limited U.S. military assistance

Table 6.1—Continued

Country	U.S. Commitment	2013 Defense Budget/Active Force	U.S. Forces	U.S. Military Cooperation
Singapore	none/UK Five-Power Agreement	$9.8 billion/72,000	4 combat ships in port	training
New Zealand	none/ANZUS Treaty suspended in 1985/declared non-NATO ally	$2.7 billion/8,500	none	2012 Washington Declaration
Malaysia	none/UK Five-Power Agreement	$5 billion/109,000	none	limited

SOURCE: IISS, 2014.

NOTE: ANZUS = Australia, New Zealand, and United States Security Treaty.

Japan has under-contributed for an array of reasons. It emerged from World War II as a pacifist nation with a U.S.-authored constitution that strictly limits its military mission to self-defense. It also sought to present itself as a peaceful nation and to avoid antagonizing its neighbors. Japan has refrained from building a nuclear weapons capability, but it remains a near–nuclear-armed power.[19] It is thus heavily dependent on the United States for its defense.

Even with these limitations, Japan has developed the most modern and well-trained armed forces in Asia, though it does not rival the PLA in size. It has about 250,000 active duty personnel and can bring modern forces to bear in a place like the Senkaku Islands. It has 47 modern naval surface combatants forming four flotillas, 18 submarines, a new helicopter carrier with a second on the way, and about 200 F-15J air superiority fighters. Japan is co-developing Standard Missile defense systems with the United States. It is slowly moving away from its decades-long static defense posture. In 2010, Japan began creating a "dynamic defense force" that stressed responsiveness and deployability, including amphibious warfare. Its new defense posture is designed to more effectively deter China and North Korea by moving forces to the southwest.[20] Tokyo also created a new National Security Council system to facilitate decisionmaking.

Prime Minister Shinzo Abe is also seeking to lift restrictions on self-defense, consistent with U.S. urging. In April 2014, Japan revised its arms-export policy to allow for greater defense cooperation with its partners. On July 1, 2014, the Japanese cabinet reinterpreted Article 9 of the constitution to allow Japan to exercise the right of collective self-defense and to expand the range of circumstances under which Japan could use its armed forces. Under this interpretation and subsequent legislation recently passed by the Diet, the Japan Self-Defense Forces can come to the aid of a partner state that is under attack if the situation would have significant consequences for Japan. Japanese forces will now be able to come to the aid of the United States and South

19 See Toshi Yoshihara and James R. Holmes, "Thinking About the Unthinkable: Tokyo's Nuclear Option," *Naval War College Review*, Vol. 62, No. 3, Summer 2009.

20 IISS, 2014, p. 250; IISS, 2012, pp. 251–255.

Korea if their forces are attacked. This will require further changes in Japanese military doctrine and force structure. It will need to develop better force-projection capabilities and operate more jointly with the United States. These are important changes that will allow Japan to become a more equal partner in Asia.

The new U.S.-Japanese Defense Guidelines—issued on April 27, 2015—will further support Japan's movement in this direction. Those guidelines are intended to provide a more "seamless, robust, flexible, and effective" bilateral response to various contingencies, including in "gray zones." The guidelines will create a new standing Alliance Coordination Mechanism to enhance bilateral planning and, specifically, add cooperation on defense equipment.[21]

In addition, Japan has sought to strengthen its security ties with Australia, India, Vietnam, the Philippines, and Indonesia. Prime Minister Abe also seeks a summit meeting with Russia to relieve some pressure on the Northern Territories issue and increase pressure on China. Further, Japan is establishing maritime hotlines with China and seeks to implement the code of Unexpected Encounters at Sea with China.[22] However, Japan's security ties with South Korea remain stalled over the issue of World War II history, the nature of Japan's apologies, and lingering bitterness over the Imperial Japanese Army's enslavement of "comfort women" before and during World War II.

If Japan is to take its place alongside the United States as a guarantor of security in East Asia and not panic its neighbors, it will need to continue to modify some policies that its neighbors consider nationalistic. Prime Minister Abe's 2013 visit to the Yasukuni Shrine, where several Japanese war criminals are interned, created a furor in both China and South Korea. Japan similarly failed to apologize adequately for atrocities that date back to World War II. Japan is criticized for the way that its history texts cover the war years and for an inadequate response to the comfort women issue. These criticisms have only become stronger over the past two decades, as China and South Korea

---

[21] Yuki Tatsumi, "4 Takeaways from the New US-Japan Defense Guidelines," *The Diplomat*, April 29, 2015.

[22] Interviews with Japanese defense officials in Tokyo, May 17–June 1, 2015.

have become more prosperous and powerful while the Japanese right wing has grown stronger. Recently, 187 Asian scholars from around the world sent an open letter to Abe asking him to face up to Japan's past.[23] Unlike Germany, Japan's neighbors—who suffered under Japanese imperialism 70 years ago—are not satisfied that Japan has repented. In Europe, Germany's handling of wartime history has allowed for a strong NATO alliance. In Asia, Japan's reticence has both created antagonism with an increasingly powerful China and prevented closer Japan-ROK ties—thus preventing multinational security arrangements like NATO's from developing.

Prime Minister Abe took an important step in correcting this problem during his 2015 speech to a joint session of Congress. He expressed "deep remorse" and "deep repentance" over Japanese actions during the war. In an August 14, 2015, cabinet statement, Abe tried to set the context for the war, emphasize Japan's peaceful role since the war, and embellish his earlier statements. He used the term "repentance" and noted that Japan had repeatedly expressed heartfelt "apology" for its actions during the war. He emphasized that the apologies articulated by previous cabinets remain unshakable, but he said that future Japanese generations should not be predestined to apologize. The Obama administration welcomed Abe's August 14 statement. Then, Emperor Akihito went beyond his annual statement to express "deep remorse." Both Seoul and Beijing were disappointed in Abe's statement because it did not represent a "full throated" apology, and South Korean President Park Geun-hye said the speech "left much to be desired."[24]

There are several steps that Japan can take in addition to the positive moves that it has made thus far to strengthen security in Asia. For example, Japan could (1) increase its defense spending beyond 1 percent of GDP, (2) take a leadership role in strengthening multilateral

---

[23] Robert Marquand, "Global 'Who's Who' of Asia Scholars Urge Japan to Own Up to WWII Atrocities," *Christian Science Monitor*, May 7, 2015.

[24] Anna Fifield, "Japan's Leader Stops Short of WWII Apology," *Washington Post*, August 14, 2015; Choe Sang-Hun, "South Korean Leader Marks Anniversary of War's End with Warnings to North Korea," *New York Times*, August 15, 2015; also see Chen Jimin, "The Paradox of Abe's Speech," *Chinausfocus.com*, August 25, 2015.

security architectures in East Asia, and (3) work with the United States and China to find a creative solution to the contending Senkaku Island claims.[25] In general, Japan needs to become a fully normal nation that spends enough on its military to defend itself against conventional attack from any neighbor.

India: Some argue that East Asia is morphing into the Indo-Pacific region. India has the potential to be an important player in East Asia. Its GDP has grown to about $2 trillion and it now possesses the third largest military in the world.[26] It is one of the world's largest arms importers and is developing a capable navy. India is a nuclear-armed power that is developing its own ballistic missiles and submarine launch capabilities. Its planned aircraft carrier fleet will allow it to project power far beyond its shores. India is also the world's largest democracy, with a long history of non-alignment. Yet it still relies most heavily on Russia for military equipment, especially fighter aircraft and naval equipment; it seeks to diversify its sources of such equipment.

India might be seen as diplomatically equidistant from Russia, China, and the United States. All three nations would benefit from drawing India closer to them. India's new prime minister, Narendra Modi, seems to be taking advantage of this fact. He is trying to improve relations with China, and invited Chinese President Xi to visit New Delhi in September and signed some 20 agreements. Modi is also considering joining the Shanghai Cooperation Organization, which is dominated by China and Russia. However, India still has border disputes with China and is growing concerned about Chinese penetration around the Indian Ocean.[27] While India's GDP is less than one-quarter that of China, it has long-term demographic advantages over China. Modi also paid a state visit to Washington to deepen that relationship and stimulate some 40 U.S.-Indian working groups. After his meeting with Obama, Modi called the United States and India "natural global

---

[25] Conclusions based on a two-week visit to Tokyo and interviews with Japanese officials from May 17 to June 1, 2015.

[26] IISS, 2012, p. 216; and IISS, 2014, p. 212.

[27] For example, India has been concerned about PLA Navy submarine visits to Colombo, Sri Lanka.

partners." Their talks focused primarily on economic issues, but they also issued a strong statement on defense cooperation, including more joint exercises and technology cooperation.[28]

India is unlikely to join any one camp exclusively—it can have more power by playing the field. The United States will need to court India enough so that India does not form tighter bonds with Russia or China than it has with the United States. Japan also has a good relationship with India and can help in this task. India may be of use in assisting the United States to moderate Chinese claims in the South China Sea. Used constructively, improved Indian-Chinese relations could help to stabilize East Asia.

The Trans-Pacific Partnership

On October 5, 2015, the United States reached agreement with 11 Pacific nations[29] on the TPP after five years of negotiation. They were stimulated by the demise of the World Trade Organization's Doha Round. These 12 nations represent about 40 percent of global GDP and 25 percent of global exports. The talks build on the 2012 South Korean–U.S. trade agreement, which is now the "gold standard" for TPP negotiations. The TPP agreement would lower trade barriers, enforce standards for labor law and and environmental law, establish a framework for intellectual property, and create a mechanism for private investor–state dispute settlement. Negotiators were unable to reach agreement on currency manipulation.[30] China is not a party to the TPP talks.

In mid-2015, President Obama was able to pass "fast-track" negotiating authority, which helped to expedite the negotiating process. Final passage in the U.S. Congress will nonetheless be problematic,

---

[28] Also see Narendra Modi and Barack Obama, "A Renewed U.S.–India Partnership for the 21st Century," *Washington Post*, September 30, 2014.

[29] Australia, Brunei, Canada, Chile, Japan, Malaysia, Mexico, New Zealand, Peru, Singapore, and Vietnam.

[30] Binnendijk, 2014a, p. 281.

given strong union and Democratic opposition to various provisions. The TPP's strategic significance will need to be weighed against its economic trade-offs when the final agreement is considered by Congress.

The TPP talks were being negotiated in parallel with the Regional Comprehensive Economic Partnership (RCEP), which includes ASEAN nations plus Australia, China, Japan, South Korea, India, and New Zealand. The RCEP talks are proceeding more slowly. In addition, the United States supported China's accession into the World Trade Organization. Linking TPP and RCEP in a hybrid arrangement could provide a powerful set of transpacific economic arrangements and, in the process, would deepen U.S.-Chinese commercial relations.[31]

The European Union lags behind the United States in negotiating trade agreements with Asia. The EU has a bilateral agreement with South Korea (2011) and has agreements under negotiation with India, Japan, Malaysia, Singapore, Thailand, and Vietnam.[32] At some future point, and in the absence of a global Doha Round, these various multilateral and bilateral agreements could be harmonized to create a comprehensive set of agreements.

The TPP agreement—combined with the other regional and global free trade talks—has significant strategic value. As the Western liberal democratic model is increasingly being challenged, providing a coherent set of economic rules for trade, investment, and services can help to strengthen the U.S. model. The TPP strengthens political, social, and economic bonds with close partners and can be part of a larger effort to manage the important U.S. relationship with China.

Military Options for Dealing with China

The United States is in the process of designing military strategies to contend with China's increasing capability to deny access to foreign naval ships within the first island chain. At least three different approaches have been identified.

---

[31] Binnendijk, 2014a, p. 282.

[32] Binnendijk, 2014a, p. 285.

The first is Air-Sea Battle, suggested by the Center for Strategic and Budgetary Assessments (CSBA), which would have U.S. forces attack command and control centers, air bases, missile launchers, submarine pens, and radar facilities on the Chinese coast that provide the strike capability China needs to deny the U.S. Navy access to the Chinese littoral. The Pentagon has recently renamed this strategy the Joint Concept for Access and Maneuver in the Global Commons, or JAM-GC. The United States is capable of executing at least part of this strategy, but it would require a high degree of preemption, a difficult political decision for any U.S. president to make when dealing with another major nuclear nation. The joint concept would be inadequate to secure military victory and would make escalation likely and war termination much more difficult.

A second strategy has been suggested by T. X. Hammes, of the National Defense University. Called Offshore Control, Hammes's strategy calls for no strikes on the Chinese mainland.[33] It envisions gaining virtual control over the South and East China seas and imposing what amounts to a naval blockade of China's major ports. It would require enough naval and air power to secure access to these two seas and to defend partner nations on the first island chain. Chinese military assets outside of its 12-mile zone would be subject to attack. Chinese commercial vessels would be boarded and stopped; cargoes could be seized. Not all commercial vessels could be boarded, but massive economic damage would be done to China, hopefully prompting policy reversals. CSBA argues that Offshore Control eschews important counterforce options that might compel China to capitulate.[34]

RAND is developing a third strategy that would mirror China's A2/AD capabilities. It would use similar technologies, primarily Army missile systems, deployed on the coastlines of U.S. partners along the

---

[33] T. X. Hammes, *Offshore Control: A Proposed Strategy for an Unlikely Conflict*, Washington, D.C.: National Defense University, Strategic Forum No. 278, June 2012.

[34] Wendell Minnick, "China Threat: Air-Sea Battle vs. Offshore Control?" *Defense News*, June 23, 2014.

first island chain. This would prevent Chinese vessels and aircraft from operating freely in the same waters.[35]

These three strategies are not mutually exclusive but—given tight defense budgets—priorities will need to be set. The consequences for the United States' partners in the region will be profound. They may be asked to participate in Air-Sea Battle, to participate in a naval blockade, or to deploy military assets designed to create A2/AD problems for China. They need to be consulted.

Potential Strategies for Managing China

Former Secretary of State Henry Kissinger has argued that a combination of deterrence and partnership is required to manage the U.S. relationship with China. In his latest book, Kissinger wrote:

> Concepts of partnership need to become, paradoxically, elements of the modern balance of power, especially in Asia—an approach that, if implemented as an overarching principle, would be as unprecedented as it is important. The combination of balance-of-power strategy with partnership diplomacy will not be able to remove all adversarial aspects, but it can mitigate their impact. Above all, it can give Chinese and American leaders experience in constructive cooperation, and convey to their two societies a way of building a more peaceful future.[36]

Kissinger essentially suggests a dual-track policy reminiscent of the 1967 Harmel Report, in which NATO set out on a new path of deterrence and détente with regard to the Soviet Union. That policy united the Alliance and put the Soviet Union on the defensive. If implemented, the Kissinger policy would at once treat China more like

---

[35] See Terrence K. Kelly, Anthony Atler, Todd Nichols, and Lloyd Thrall, *Employing Land-Based Anti-Ship Missiles in the Western Pacific*, Santa Monica, Calif.: RAND Corporation, TR-1321-A, 2013, and David Ochmanek, *Sustaining U.S. Leadership in the Asia-Pacific Region: Why a Strategy of Direct Defense Against Antiaccess and Area Denial Threats Is Desirable and Feasible*, Santa Monica, Calif.: RAND Corporation, PE-142-OSD, 2015.

[36] Henry Kissinger, *World Order*, New York: Penguin Press, September 2014b, p. 233.

a great power while organizing its regional neighbors to provide a more adequate strategic balance against Chinese power.

A recent Council on Foreign Relations Task Force report also suggests a dual-track approach, but with a greater emphasis on the first track, deterrence. The report recommends

> a new U.S. policy of balancing China that would in effect change the balance of current U.S. policy, in the process placing less emphasis on support and cooperation and more on pressure and competition. There would be less hedging and more active countering.[37]

That suggested policy, however, would heighten China's sense that the United States seeks to encircle it, making the second track more difficult to implement. It would run counter to the policies of many U.S. partners in Asia and Europe, and it would risk pushing China closer to Russia.

To implement a balanced dual-track policy with China, the United States would need to strengthen both the "cooperation" track and the "countering" track. On the partnership side, the United States might begin by pursuing precisely what China means by establishing a "new type of great power relationship" and determine whether this can be accomplished without abandoning U.S. partners. It might also press to include China in the TPP talks at an appropriate moment. It might reverse course and join the new Chinese-inspired AIIB. It might design a mutually acceptable procedure for avoiding maritime conflicts and settling maritime disputes. The United States is, admittedly, at a disadvantage on the second item for not having ratified the UN Convention on the Law of the Seas. It might establish clearer pre-notification procedures for maritime activities in the East and South China seas and rules of the road for military behavior. An important step in this direction was taken in November 2014, when the United States and China agreed to confidence-building measures for voluntary notifica-

---

[37] Robert D. Blackwill and Ashley J. Tellis, *Revising U.S. Grand Strategy Toward China*, Washington, D.C.: Council on Foreign Relations, Council Special Report No. 72, March 2015.

tion of major military activities and for a code of conduct for safe maritime and air encounters. These two agreements are not yet fully implemented, but they represent constructive efforts to avoid incidents that might escalate into unwanted conflict.[38]

To make a higher degree of partnership work, the United States and China would need to go beyond the current Strategic and Economic Dialogue talks, which produce practical coöperative steps, in an effort to dispel fundamental distrust that exists between them. Continuation of presidential-level discussions started at Sunnylands aimed not at incremental agreements but at correcting fundamental misperceptions on both sides will be critical to this process.

Figure 6.4 describes how the two sides see each other. It also suggests a different "objective reality" in both cases. For partnership to really work, each side must move away from its stereotypical views of the other.

At the same time, the United States must pursue the deterrence track and make it as multilateral as possible. It has already shifted forces to Asia, strengthened basing arrangements throughout the area, and bolstered bilateral relations. It is modernizing its nuclear forces and protecting Defense Department cyber networks. It should continue to develop a full spectrum of defense strategies and capabilities and not rely on just an Air-Sea Battle Strategy that could trap a future U.S. president into choosing an unpalatable course of action. The United States must also defend the security interests of its treaty allies without letting those partners draw it into unwanted conflict. That requires a high degree of policy coordination with Asian partners.

The difficult task for the United States is to strengthen each track without dislodging the other. Excessive exuberance over a new strategic partnership could lead to defense budget cuts that could undermine deterrence. Excessive deterrence would feed Chinese paranoia about encirclement.

---

[38] Mira Rapp-Hooper and Bonnie Glaser, "In Confidence: Will We Know If US-China CMBs Are Working?" *Asia Maritime Transparency Initiative* blog post, Center for Strategic and International Studies, February 4, 2015.

Figure 6.4
Subjective and Objective Models of Reality

China

Chinese Subjective View

China has incontestable sovereign claims that it must assert now that it has the strength to do so. The United States may try to deny those interests, encircle China, and threaten the Chinese homeland. Yet growing Chinese A2/AD capabilities and sagging U.S. ones will work to China's advantage in a crisis. If war occurs, it can be brief and successful if China disables U.S. strike forces before they can be used.

"Objective" View

Other states in the region do not accept the primacy of Chinese claims just because China now has more strength to enforce them. The United States would welcome China as a powerful but restrained force in East Asia. U.S. concern for regional stability does not imply creation of an anti-China alignment. At the same time, the United States has the will to use or sustain force to defend its interests, its allies, and freedom of the seas. Sino-U.S. conflict might not end quickly.

United States

U.S. Subjective View

China aspires to make East Asia its exclusive sphere of influence. If allowed, it will use its growing military power to intimidate its neighbors and enforce its terms. Allies and others will lose faith in the United States if it does not back them and their claims. Chinese A2/AD capabilities are vulnerable; if destroyed before they can be used, conflict with China could be swift, low-cost, and successful.

"Objective" View

China wants to advance what it deems its rightful territorial claims. It may seek to intimidate, but not to conquer, its neighbors. Expanding regional alliances will be read by China as encirclement. China's fear of U.S. force projection and strike capabilities is its main motivation for developing A2/AD. China's will to defend its interests is considerable. Sino-U.S. conflict could take unpredictable and dangerous paths.

SOURCE: Gompert, Binnendijk, and Lin, 2014.
RAND *RR1210-6.4*

A Regional Strategy for Asia

As the Middle East and Ukraine top the international news, Asia continues to grow as a center of economic and political power. The combination of potential flash points plus lack of adequate security architecture to manage conflict and escalation makes Asia a dangerous place for U.S. interests. Should major conflict break out with North Korea or China, the consequences could be catastrophic for the United States.

In that sense, the U.S. pivot to Asia continues to make some analytical sense despite the difficulties in implementing it. The principal U.S. focus in Asia must be to manage the rise of China while protecting U.S. partners.

The United States has a fundamental stake in finding peaceful solutions to the multiple maritime disputes in the South and East China seas. It needs to take a more active role to establish an agreed process to solve these disputes. Some bridge needs to be found between China's desire to negotiate bilaterally and U.S. partners' desire to negotiate multilaterally.

North Korea remains on a dangerous trajectory as its technology increasingly threatens the United States directly. Deterrence will remain critical on the peninsula. Washington and Seoul need to fully coordinate any responses to aggression from Pyongyang and consultations with China are needed to coordinate activities should there be a sudden collapse of the regime in Pyongyang.

The Asian security architecture needs to be multilateralized by encouraging Japan, South Korea, and Australia to develop greater political cohesion and military interoperability. Political reconciliation between Tokyo and Seoul and closer ties among these three countries and with NATO are needed.

At the same time, ASEAN and the ARF need to be strengthened. That could serve as a building block for an Organization for Security and Cooperation in Europe–like organization that would include China.

The TPP trade agreement would have broad value beyond trade and could bind the United States' partners more closely together. TPP could also help assimilate an emerging China if it is allowed to join.

Europe can play a more constructive role in Asia beyond trade. Europe can serve as a model in Asia for institution-building, norm-setting, and reconciliation. The United States and the EU need to coordinate their policies toward Asia more carefully and form closer trilateral ties with Asian partners. NATO should extend enhanced opportunity partnerships to Japan and South Korea, thus linking those countries more closely to both Australia and NATO.

As India emerges as a great power in Asia, its strategic orientation will be critical. Rapprochement between India and China need not be at the expense of the United States. If properly managed, it could help bring greater stability to Asia.

There is little room in Asia today for U.S. retrenchment—the entire region depends too heavily on U.S. security commitments. Should the United States appear to be reneging on those commitments, Japan and South Korea would likely develop nuclear weapons fairly quickly. Weaker nations would have no choice but to accede to Chinese will. China would take advantage by pressing its maritime claims even further. On the other hand, excessive assertiveness in protecting the maritime claims of others would make a degree of rapprochement with China even more difficult.

A collaborative approach to security in Asia seems most productive: It would retain U.S. force levels in Asia at current levels; it would concentrate primarily on Japan, encouraging Japan's recent efforts to play a larger regional security role; it might press Japan to spend more on defense and urge Japan to seek greater accommodation with South Korea by reducing historical animosity; it would seek to bring Indian power into the East Asian equation to help balance China; and it would engage China in an effort to defuse the dangerous situation in the East and South China seas and to create an agreed mechanism for settling contending maritime claims.

CHAPTER SEVEN

In Search of a Middle East Partnership Strategy

The United States has historically had three fundamental interests in the Middle East: to provide security for Israel, to guarantee the free flow of Persian Gulf oil to the West, and to counter Soviet efforts during the Cold War to undermine U.S. influence in the region. That meant supporting moderate Arab regimes, regardless of their commitment to democracy. After 1978, another U.S. interest was to limit Iranian power. Since September 11, 2001, those interests have been overshadowed by efforts to defeat terrorists who could threaten the United States and by a new emphasis on preventing the proliferation of weapons of mass destruction. These circumstances were accompanied by a new emphasis on democracy promotion in the region.

Until 2001, U.S. national security strategy was not defined by its Middle East policy, as the region generally took a back seat to events in Europe and Asia. At times, the United States intervened in the Middle East with military force, but generally it supported partners in the region indirectly. During the Cold War, the United States successfully prevented the Soviet Union from unraveling Israeli victories in the 1967 and 1973 wars. Two fundamental changes transpired during the Carter administration, one positive and one negative. The Camp David Accords removed the single most important threat to Israel and set up mechanisms under which the United States still provides a combined total of about $5 billion annually to Israel and Egypt. On the other hand, U.S. support for the Shah of Iran led to the 1979 hostage crisis and 35 years of tense relations. Policy under the Reagan administration was akin to what some now call "offshore balancing," under which the

United States supported Saddam Hussein's Iraq as a surrogate against Iran. Iraq's invasion of Kuwait led to a dramatic shift in U.S. policy and to Operation Desert Storm, the first major U.S. military intervention in the region since World War II. The Clinton administration maintained no-fly zones in Iraq but generally sought to deemphasize U.S. military involvement.

That all changed after 9/11. Two wars and costly decade-long stabilization operations in Iraq and Afghanistan involved the United States in the Middle East more heavily than ever before. The Obama administration's pivot to Asia sought to end those long military engagements. If military force became necessary, it was to be surgical, with partners, and of short duration. A critical question for future U.S. strategy is the degree of military involvement that the United States is willing to maintain.

The Middle East Today

Military conflict with Putin's Russia or Xi's China presents potential existential threats to the United States. That risk is small but cannot be ignored. Threats from the Middle East can reach the U.S. homeland and certainly U.S. interests abroad. They can threaten U.S. cities if terrorists can acquire and deliver weapons of mass destruction. They can disrupt international transportation and threaten U.S. citizens and partners. Threats from the Middle East are not existential, yet they are urgent. Avoiding existential threats from China and Russia is, in a larger sense, more important.

President Obama sought to capture this notion in a September 2013 United Nations General Assembly speech in which he highlighted four U.S. core interests in the region. Those essential interests were a result of a summer 2013 policy reassessment. Obama declared that the United States would

- confront external aggression against our allies and partners (including Israel)
- ensure the free flow of energy from the region to the world

- dismantle terrorist networks that threaten Americans and U.S. allies
- not tolerate the development or use of weapons of mass destruction.[1]

Obama's definition of U.S. interests included the two traditional imperatives of protecting oil and Israel as well as the post-9/11 concerns of terrorists and weapons of mass destruction. Obama did not highlight human rights or democracy as did presidents Jimmy Carter and George W. Bush. While Obama supported democracy building in the region, he noted that democracy cannot be imposed by force. These core interests in the Middle East are consistent with an interest-based, rather than a value-based, foreign policy. In that sense, they represent a narrowing that is consistent with Obama's overall foreign policy of restraint. Since increased tension with Russia and China could pose existential threats to the United States, that narrowing of core interests in the Middle East seems practical.

And yet, it is in the Middle East that the Obama administration has come in for its greatest foreign policy criticism. These criticisms have been levied for

- withdrawing U.S. troops from Iraq prematurely
- announcing withdrawal plans for Afghanistan while implementing a surge
- failing to use airstrikes against Syria after drawing a "red line" under the use of chemical weapons
- failing to provide stabilization operations for Libya and greater security for embassy personnel there
- attacking ISIS while pledging not to use U.S. ground combat forces
- supporting the Muslim Brotherhood's elected President Mohamed Morsi in Egypt and then supporting a subsequent military coup
- agreeing to a nuclear accord with Iran that some see as flawed

---

[1] Evan McMorris-Santoro, "Obama Lays Out America's 'Core Interests' in the Middle East," *Buzzfeed News*, September 24, 2013.

- pressing Israel too hard on its settlements policy.

Most relate to Obama's efforts to end two wars in the Middle East, his policy of restraint in engaging there again with U.S. ground forces, his efforts to negotiate a halt to Iran's nuclear program, and his efforts to negotiate peace between Israel and Palestinians. These policies are the by-product of efforts to moderate the assertive policies of the George W. Bush administration.

Vulnerable American Partners

The fuse for Arab Spring was lit in 2010 by the self-immolation of Tunisian fruit seller Mohamed Bouazizi, but the hope that the popular response would ignite a democratic transformation throughout the region quickly fizzled. Tunisia is one of the few Arab states that has become a relatively stable democracy as a result. Elsewhere, the result has been anarchy, instability, or a return to authoritarian government. The ensuing chaos has created great difficulty not only for the region but also for U.S. foreign policy. There is no proven formula for dealing with the results.

One might categorize the states in the Middle East into three groups: those in active civil war or anarchy, those that are still stable but more vulnerable, and those that have emerged with some degree of stability.

Libya, Afghanistan, Iraq, Syria, and Yemen are in the first group. In Libya, Afghanistan, and Iraq, the United States promoted regime change through military operations, whereas in Syria and Yemen it generally supported regime change. The result has been change for the worse. The civil war in Syria has been most brutal, with over 200,000 casualties and more than three million refugees. The war has divided the region primarily according to religious affiliation. Shi'ites in Iran and Iraq and Hezbollah have supported the Assad regime, while Sunni states in the Gulf, Jordan, Egypt, and Turkey have tended to support the opposition—in some cases, Sunni extremists. Libya is in a state of near anarchy, with regional militias vying for control. Afghanistan and Iraq are both new democracies torn by civil war and insurgency. Houthi Shi'ite rebels have swept through Yemen, which Saudi Arabia has countered with an air war; as of this writing, the Houthis are in control of most of the country. Syria, Iraq, and Yemen could each divide into separate states.

A second group of countries that are more vulnerable today includes Jordan, Lebanon, and Bahrain—all nations historically important to the United States. Large numbers of Syrian refugees risk overwhelming the capacity of Jordan and Lebanon and destabilizing those nations. Larger international efforts may be needed to help manage the refugee crisis there. In the case of Bahrain, its Sunni government and Shi'ite majority are unable to agree on more representational government, and the homeport of the U.S. Fifth Fleet is at risk.

The third group includes those states that have weathered the storm thus far, though none is without serious internal problems. These include three non-Arab countries (Turkey, Pakistan, and Iran), Egypt, Saudi Arabia, the United Arab Emirates, Oman, Morocco, Tunisia, and Algeria. Most have survived by cracking down on dissidents, Islamist radicals, and the Muslim Brotherhood. For those in this group that are at least democracies in name, the democratic process has—to varying degrees—been sacrificed for stability. For those in this group that are monarchies, they have generally promoted just enough reform for the regime to survive.

Five years of this rollercoaster ride have created deep problems for U.S. foreign policy. For example, in Egypt, after the overthrow of President Hosni Mubarak, Washington was determined to support free democratic elections, but those elections brought Muslim Brotherhood leader Morsi to power. He sought to move Egypt away from secularism. That disastrous policy was followed by anti-Morsi protests and a military coup. The United States was criticized first for supporting Islamists and then for supporting military rule. Yet U.S. policy had little impact on events in Egypt, and its influence in the Middle East in general is in decline. Casimir Yost concluded in a summer 2014 article in *The American Interest* that:

> The United States is experiencing a strategic reversal of its once-prominent position in the Middle East. It is fast becoming just another squabbling player on a chaotic and complex game board. This reversal has been years in the making but has clearly accelerated since U.S. troops left Iraq and since they began to leave Afghanistan. For the United States, this diminished status is humbling. For the region, it is deeply unsettling.
>
> The agent of America's shrunken regional role is not another state but rather the chaos spreading from Tripoli to Lahore.[2]

Layers of Chaos and Contradiction

This chaos is multifaceted. In some places states are not only failing but dissolving, further complicating U.S. decisionmaking. In this turmoil, it is often difficult to find partners that generally align with U.S. interests or values. Simple dividing lines like pro- or anti-communism or even authoritarian or democratic no longer apply. Partners that receive billions of dollars of U.S. assistance or arms often pursue policies directly at odds with the United States. Sometimes, even adversaries such as Iran find common interest with the United States.

The fractured landscape includes the following types of conflicts:

- Sunni versus Shi'a
- Democratic versus authoritarian
- Authoritarian versus the Muslim Brotherhood and other Islamists
- Arab versus Persian
- Arab versus Israel
- All versus ISIS.[3]

If one layer of complexity results in a temporary partnership of convenience on one set of issues, other layers could soon undermine those common interests.

---

[2] Casmir Yost, "Out of the Quicksand," *The American Interest*, Vol. 9, No. 5, 2014, p. 96.

[3] This list reflects the thinking of James Dobbins

The Sunni versus Shi'a split dates back to the 7th century, but it has intensified in the wake of conflict in Iraq, Syria, Yemen, and Bahrain. The split has been most pronounced where a minority rules a majority. For example, under Saddam Hussein, the Sunni minority ruled the Shi'ite majority; now that the tables are reversed, the Shi'ite majority seems unable to share power with their former persecutors. In Syria, the small Alawite (Shi'a) minority under Assad has clung to power over a Sunni majority; ISIS is one result. In Bahrain, the Sunni minority backed by Saudi Arabia has struggled to hold on to power. One great danger for the Middle East now is further regionalization of Sunni-Shi'a conflict with state-sponsored support for both sides. This raises the analogy to Europe's Thirty Years' War, which some fear is now unfolding in the Middle East. The map in Figure 7.1 shows these divisions in detail.

Since 1979, the United States has tended to support Sunni leadership in the Gulf and throughout the Middle East. Yet Sunni Islamist

Figure 7.1
Muslim Population Map: Shi'ites as a Percentage of the Muslim Population

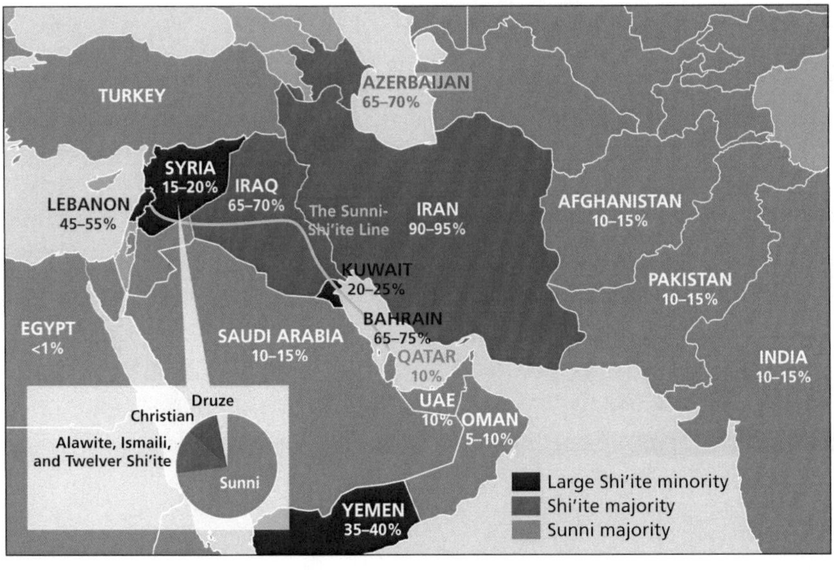

SOURCES: Pew Research Center, U.S. Department of State.
RAND *RR1210-7.1*

groups, such as Hamas, al Qaeda, Jabhat al-Nusra, and now ISIS, are public enemy number one. The United States has opposed Shi'ite Iran and Hezbollah for four decades, but now there is common cause with them against ISIS.

As James Dobbins has noted, "democratization is not a binary condition."[4] Many nations in the greater Middle East can claim some degree of democracy, however cosmetic. Iraq, Afghanistan, Pakistan, and Egypt have electoral processes. Many of the region's monarchies have elected parliaments. Even theocratic Iran holds elections that can bring substantial change. The split between those countries that are more democratic and those who are more authoritarian does not seem to present a major dividing line in the Middle East.

With regard to the Muslim Brotherhood and Iran, RAND's Dalia Dassa Kaye made the following observations:

> Even our regional partners are themselves divided on how to approach the regional transformations underway. The Egyptians, Saudis and Emiratis are taking the lead in outlawing and ultimately attempting to eradicate the Muslim Brotherhood, while some of their Gulf neighbors like Qatar continue to support political Islamist forces and offer a safe haven for fleeing Muslim Brotherhood leaders. Turkey, a NATO ally, is still run by a Muslim Brotherhood affiliated political party. . . . The approach to Iran also creates fissures among American allies, with some partners like Turkey and Oman taking more accommodating positions (and even helping to mediate direct U.S.-Iranian dialogue) while others, led by the Saudis, maintain deep-rooted suspicions and fear of Iranian regional ambitions.[5]

Unlike in Europe or Asia, alignments in the Middle East are much more temporary, based on which conflict is most prevalent at any given time. The coalition against ISIS is a case in point. By late September 2014, the United States had assembled more than 60 global coalition partners, including a strong Arab group, to make clear that

---

[4] Dobbins et al., 2015.

[5] Dalia Dassa Kaye, personal communication with the author, June 25, 2014.

this was not a Western attack on Sunni Arabs. Arab coalition partners included Iraq, Lebanon, Jordan, Bahrain, Saudi Arabia, the United Arab Emirates, Kuwait, Qatar, Egypt, Oman, Morocco, Tunisia, and the Arab League. Turkey was a non-Arab Muslim partner, while Iran was a tacit partner. The Syrian government also gains from this coalition because its most capable domestic opponent is the primary target. While this is a potentially powerful coalition, it is unclear if it will have the desired result on the battlefield and if it could be assembled for another purpose.

Pivotal Partners: Israel, Egypt, Saudi Arabia, Pakistan

Israel, Egypt, Saudi Arabia, and Pakistan have traditionally been strong U.S. partners in the region but, for varying reasons, all four partnerships have become troubled. A common concern is that the U.S. pivot toward Asia and associated restraint in the Middle East and South Asia will undercut the security of these nations. Restoring these relationships without excessively remilitarizing U.S. policy in the region needs to be a critical element of U.S. grand strategy.

Israel: The U.S. partnership with Israel is based on more than half a century of close and personal ties. While no formal security treaty exists, Washington's underlying commitment to Israel has been reiterated by every U.S. president. Nonetheless, squabbles among the closest friends take place, as has been the case recently between the United States and Israel. There have been several causes.

The first is the contours of a peace settlement. Despite significant efforts by U.S. Secretary of State John Kerry, efforts to find a diplomatic solution between Israel and Palestinians have not been unsuccessful. Peace negotiations that dominated much of Middle East politics for decades have receded in apparent importance. Israel, on the one hand, might feel more secure with the Egyptian and Jordanian peace agreements still holding and other dangerous neighbors like Syria and Iraq in turmoil. But if that instability dislodges the current governments in Amman and Cairo, those agreements could become vulnerable. Thus, there are differing interpretations of Israeli security today. In May 2011,

Obama suggested that Israel would need to accept the pre-1967 borders for a peace settlement to be successful. Prime Minister Benjamin Netanyahu responded that those borders were "indefensible."

Related to that is Israel's settlement policy, which the Obama administration believes undercuts the prospects for peace talks with Palestinians. That U.S. theme was first sounded during Obama's 2009 speech in Cairo, where he said that "the United States does not accept the legitimacy of continued Israeli settlements."[6]

Another area of conflict is the Iranian nuclear program. Netanyahu and Obama both have set red lines for Iran's nuclear program, but those red lines are different. Netanyahu's relate to a level of uranium enrichment, while Obama's relate to development of a nuclear weapon. Netanyahu went directly to the U.S. Congress and the American people to state his concerns about the nuclear deal with Iran. Those efforts have continues since an agreement was reached. The final Vienna agreement will deepen those divisions.

Finally, there is personal animosity between the two leaders. In November 2011, Obama and French President Nicholas Sarkozy were overheard complaining about Netanyahu. During the 2012 U.S. presidential elections, Netanyahu openly embraced Republican nominee Mitt Romney.[7] Nonetheless, when the going gets tough, as was the case with Palestinian statehood in the UN, the United States has supported Israel's interests.

Israel and the United States share common goals, common cultural values, an interest in stabilizing the Middle East, and support for a halt to nuclear proliferation. Despite some current differences in how to implement common goals, it is in the interest of both countries to strengthen ties. The November 2015 meeting between Obama and Netanyahu was a pragmatic and important step in that direction.

Egypt: After the Camp David Accords, Egypt became the United States' closest partner in the Arab world. From 1948 to 2014, Egypt received $75 billion in U.S. foreign aid. Its military is equipped

---

[6] Barack Obama, "Text: Obama's Speech in Cairo," *New York Times*, June 4, 2009.

[7] Aliyah Frumin, "Obama's Rocky Relationship with Israel: A Timeline," *MSNBC.com*, September 13, 2013.

with advanced U.S. weapons, and Egypt's military officers were often trained by the United States. Egyptian officers were in close touch with American colleagues during the demonstrations against President Mubarak, and military restraint was due in part to American advice. However, most Egyptian officers believe that the United States moved too quickly to abandon Mubarak. After a year of Muslim Brotherhood rule, the Egyptian military overthrew and imprisoned President Morsi without the full support of the United States. The subsequent violence is estimated to have cost 2,500 lives. Most Muslim Brotherhood leaders are in jail or hiding. Insurgencies have erupted in the Sinai peninsula and pro-military judges have sentenced Muslim Brotherhood members to death. Protest laws bar unauthorized gatherings of more than ten people.

A degree of stability has been reestablished and the bloody civil war predicted by some has not materialized. The Obama administration has sought to take a middle-ground position. In his May 2014 West Point commencement speech, Obama said: "We acknowledge that our relationship is anchored in security interests. . . . So we have not cut off cooperation . . . but we can and will persistently press for reforms."[8] While U.S. Central Command sees Egypt as vital to U.S. national security interests, many in the Egyptian military are bitter about U.S. policies. The March 2015 decision to resume $1.3 billion in U.S. annual military aid—which had been suspended following the coup—may improve that situation.[9] Both nations share a common interest in defeating religious extremists, which is a solid foundation on which to strengthen relations.

Saudi Arabia: The United States and Saudi Arabia are unlikely partners. One is the world's most powerful democracy, while the other is the world's most absolute monarchy. Yet for most of the past seven decades, they have shared a symbiotic relationship: Saudi Arabia pro-

---

[8] Barack Obama, "Remarks by the President at the United States Military Academy Commencement Ceremony," West Point, N.Y.: The White House, Office of the Press Secretary, May 28, 2014.

[9] See Jeremy M. Sharp, *Egypt: Background and U.S. Relations*, Washington, D.C.: Congressional Research Service, RL33003, June 5, 2014.

vided oil and the United States provided security. Saudi Arabia has about one-fifth of the world's proven oil reserves and produces about 10 million barrels per day. It has often used flexible production to stabilize oil markets, much to the United States' benefit. The United States decided in the late 1970s and early 1980s to sell F-15s and AWACS (Airborne Warning and Control System) jets to Saudi Arabia. Those aircraft and related facilities were critical for coalition forces during Operation Desert Storm, which was fought in large measure to protect Saudi oil fields from Saddam Hussein. Now the United States has overtaken Saudi Arabia as the world's largest oil producer, Saudi markets are shifting to Europe and Asia, and security relations have frayed over Iran. Peter Bergen concluded in March 2014 that the relationship "has never been in worse shape."[10]

After 9/11, the Saudis seemed duplicitous, as 15 of their citizens were found to be prominent in the 9/11 attacks and Saudi private funds subsidized Wahhabi radical groups associated with al Qaeda. Subsequently, the Saudis did crack down on financing for al Qaeda. But democracy-promotion advocates in the United States continue to look with suspicion at the Saudi monarchy.

The Saudis are highly concerned about the Vienna nuclear accord with Iran. They are anxious about the spread of Iranian influence into Iraq, Syria, Bahrain, Lebanon, and Yemen and fear that U.S.-Iranian rapprochement will put Saudi Arabia at a significant disadvantage with its Iranian rival. Saudis were also shocked by the speed with which Obama abandoned Mubarak, a longtime Saudi ally, and the fact that Obama did not use airpower to unseat Assad in Syria.

Saudi King Salman's decision to shift the royal line of succession to his close relatives may portend some long-term stability in U.S.-Saudi relations. Prince Mohammed bin Nayef, the new crown prince, has cooperated closely with the United States on counterterrorism operations, but the shift may also portend future instability within the Saudi royal family.

President Obama visited Riyadh in March 2014 in an attempt to improve relations while the rise of ISIS gives the two nations a

[10] Peter Bergen, "Why the Saudis Unfriended the U.S.," *CNN.com*, March 28, 2014.

common enemy. The United States has also collaborated recently with Saudi bombing operations in Yemen, but the relationship remains awkward.[11] The Saudi King decided to decline Obama's invitation to attend a Camp David meeting designed to reassure Sunni leaders about the United States' shifting ties with Iran.

After the agreement was reached in Vienna on the Iran nuclear deal, the United States has successfully sought ways to gain tacit Saudi acceptance. The United States will need to demonstrate that it has not shifted its fundamental alignment toward Tehran.

Pakistan: The United States and Pakistan also had a close partnership during the Cold War, with Pakistan a member of the Central Treaty Organization (CENTO).[12] The United States provided advanced weapons to Pakistan, as did China, but, by 2013, former Pakistani Ambassador to the United States Husain Haqqani was calling the relationship "toxic."[13]

Relations began to change in the 1980s, when Pakistan embarked on a nuclear weapons program in an effort to maintain a degree of parity with regional rival India. In 1985, Congress passed the Pressler Amendment, which sought to halt Pakistani proliferation by requiring the U.S. president to certify each year that Pakistan did not possess nuclear weapons. By 1990, it was no longer possible to make that certification, and most military aid and training was cut. The Pakistani military felt betrayed. In 1995, those U.S. restrictions were partially lifted but the damage was done.[14] During the past decade, the United States continued to provide Pakistan with about $1.3 billion in foreign aid annually.

---

[11] "Awkward Relations," *The Economist*, March 29, 2014.

[12] The United States was not a member of CENTO but was represented in its military committee.

[13] Sara Carter, "Pakistan Is No Ally of the U.S. and the 'Toxic' Relationship Threatens National Security: Former Pakistani Ambassador," *The Blaze*, December 2, 2013.

[14] As a staffer for the Senate Foreign Relations Committee, the author was heavily involved with the Pressler Amendment while it was being considered in the U.S. Senate. See "August 1985: Pressler Amendment Passed, Requiring Yearly Certification that Pakistan Does Not Have Nuclear Weapons," HistoryCommons.org, undated.

By 2011, new issues arose to create one of the worst years in U.S.-Pakistan relations.[15] Central Intelligence Agency contractor Raymond Davis killed two Pakistanis in Lahore who were following him. Then, Osama Bin Laden was killed by U.S. Navy Seals in his Abbottabad safe house near the Pakistani Military Academy. Both sides cried foul. Next, a flawed NATO attack on a Pakistani military outpost near the border with Afghanistan killed 24 soldiers, in what the United States claimed was an error but Pakistani generals deeply believed was retaliation. Underlying this tension was the war in Afghanistan.

Since the low point in 2011, bilateral relations have been gradually improving under Prime Minister Nawaz Sharif and U.S. Ambassador Richard Olsen.[16] For example, Pakistan has engaged in a yearlong effort to clear Islamists from the Shawal Valley, from which they were attacking U.S. troops in Afghanistan.[17] Over time, the United States will need to convince Pakistan that India will not encircle it in the wake of U.S. withdrawals. Pakistan will need to realize that the Taliban (both Afghan and Pakistani) is a threat to Pakistan itself and that threat must be eliminated. Meanwhile, the United States and Pakistan have a common interest in preventing further conflict with India, and a U.S. initiative there might improve relations with Islamabad considerably.

Russia Joins the Fray

President Putin's decision to come to Syrian President Assad's aid in the fall of 2015 has further complicated the Middle East equation. Much will depend on U.S. and Russian willingness to coordinate their diplomacy and operations. Risks include deeper sectarian splits if the Russia-Shi'a coalition and the U.S.-Sunni coalition fight a proxy war

---

[15] Shehzad H. Qazi, "US-Pakistan Relations: Common and Clashing Interests," *World Affairs*, May/June 2012.

[16] Ayaz Gul, "Olson: US-Pakistan Relations Still Challenging, Improving," *Voice of America*, February 3, 2014.

[17] Tim Craig, "Pakistani Military Says It Achieved Major Victory in Mountain Assault," *Washington Post*, July 4, 2015.

in Syria. That could lead to incidents between U.S. and Russian forces, which defense ministries are trying to prevent through deconfliction. However, advantages also exist if Russia and the United States can agree to focus their air strikes on ISIS—and perhaps al Nusra Front—targets and to shape a political solution at the Vienna talks.

Russia and the United States have a common interest in defeating ISIS quickly and in preventing a radical Islamist state from emerging in Damascus. They disagree on the importance of protecting the Assad government, and hence on targeting air strikes.

Enough common interest exists between the United States and Russia in Syria to reach a compromise. The recent ISIS attacks on Paris and on the Russian airliner should strengthen these common interests. If Russia would agree to limit its air strikes to primarily ISIS targets, the United States might agree to allow Assad to participate in transition talks to form a new Alawite-Sunni coalition government, to be formed without him.[18]

The ability of the United States and Russia to recognize and act on their common interests will have a profound impact on the future shape of the Middle East.

Alternatives for a New Middle East Strategy

The U.S. strategy for Europe is fairly clear-cut: to unite allies, shift the defense burden, coerce Russia to behave differently, and deter Russia from incursions into NATO territory. The U.S. strategy for Asia will depend on whether it can strengthen its security relationships with allies and still find a new balance with China. A regional strategy for the Middle East is the least clear cut. It must seek to contain the consequences of the violent chaos that currently exists in the region without drawing the United States in so deeply that it is unable to focus on challenges of greater strategic relevance in Europe and Asia.

---

[18] The Vienna process, started in October 2015, includes 19 nations and will seek a ceasefire and political solution to the Syria conflict. Participants include the United States, key European partners, Russia, Iran, and Saudi Arabia. If these parties can agree, they can construct a diplomatic solution to the Syria conflict.

U.S. partnerships in the Middle East are, in general, much more fluid than those in Europe and Asia. The United States has been able to assemble a significant coalition of Arab states to fight ISIS. In addition to that primarily Sunni coalition, the United States is working in parallel with Tehran and even Damascus to accomplish its stated mission of degrading and eventually defeating ISIS. That coalition will probably not extend too far beyond the fight against ISIS. The multiple layers of conflict, chaos, and resulting contradictions will make it difficult for the United States to do more than create ad hoc coalitions when needed.

With this degree of uncertainty, the United States can take several broad approaches to deal with its partners in the Middle East. These are neither comprehensive nor mutually exclusive.

First, the United States could focus primarily on rebuilding its traditional strong partnerships with Sunni governments in Egypt, Saudi Arabia, Israel, and Pakistan. This path would maximize U.S. influence in the region to mitigate future contingencies. The goal would be to focus on fighting extremism and promoting stability in the region.

Second, the United States could seek to construct a more cooperative relationship with Iran. This would build on the Vienna nuclear agreement and cooperation against ISIS to establish a broader set of regional approaches to the Middle East. It would assume a degree of willingness on the part of Iran to limit its support of Shi'a extremism and confrontation with U.S. Sunni allies. This path could fundamentally change the political equation in the Middle East, but it would also create significant unrest among the United States' Sunni partners and meet substantial U.S. domestic opposition. Strengthening ties with both the dominant Shi'a state and leading Sunni states would be a difficult diplomatic balancing act. It would probably require clearer military assurances to Iran's neighbors and continuing opposition to Iran's policies in Syria and Yemen—but the rewards could be great. It could place the United States in a better position to limit the prospects of a region-wide sectarian conflict.

Third, the United States might focus on counterterrorism and nuclear non-proliferation as its principal efforts. These are two of the four key U.S. interests listed by the Obama administration. Following them explicitly could lead to the commitment of more U.S. ground units to defeat ISIS and possibly to conflict with Iran, should implementation of the nuclear agreement falter.

Finally, the United States could focus on fundamental U.S. values like democratization and respect for universal human rights, on the theory that the Middle East is unlikely to stabilize without rights-respecting governance. That might entail reducing military cooperation with states such as Egypt, Saudi Arabia, and Pakistan and focusing instead on economic assistance. This strategy has been followed by several U.S administrations and has been generally unsuccessful. It has alienated allies and led to civil war in nations where the United States sought regime change. Nonetheless, Washington could continue this policy, perhaps with a lighter hand and a longer time horizon.

If the United States can simultaneously rebuild its relationships with its major Sunni partners and establish a more constructive relationship with Iran (approaches one and two), it might seek to design a new balance for its Middle East policies based on these pillars. That would be difficult to implement. However, if successful, it could begin to replicate the historical situation in which the United States was trusted by both Israel and Egypt and thus able to facilitate a peace treaty between them. The Obama administration seems to be testing this path by reaching agreement with Iran on its nuclear program and loosely coordinating operations against ISIS while simultaneously trying to reassure Sunni leaders and provide them with advanced weapons. If the nuclear deal with Iran is successfully implemented, the United States might also launch new regional initiatives, including a broader regional security summit that includes Iran. Increased positive Iranian engagement with the Gulf Cooperation Council will be particularly important. Continued sectarian divides are a losing proposition for people in the region and for U.S. regional interests.

The assertive policies of the George W. Bush administration were inadequate to deal with the complexity of the Middle East and led to two costly and largely unsuccessful wars. The Obama policies of restraint in the Middle East echo elements of the Offshore Balancing strategy, for which there may still be a role in the region. However, those Obama policies have also been heavily criticized for "leading from behind" and opening the door to greater anarchy in the region. A collaborative policy based on balancing ties with both long-time Sunni partners and with Iran may prove to be equally frustrating. The tension between closer ties with Iran and maintaining the trust of Sunni leaders is clear, but if a new balance can be found, it could place the United States on a stronger footing with key partners and provide a framework for avoiding greater sectarian conflict throughout the region.

CHAPTER EIGHT

Conclusion: Choosing an Approach

The U.S. rebalance or pivot to Asia is the closest thing that the Obama administration has offered to a grand strategy. That made sense when the policy was issued. However, as discussed in the preceding chapters, the international environment has become more dangerous since the pivot strategy was designed. The United States now faces at least five potential adversaries at a time when defense budgets are declining. To meet these challenges, the United States will need to defeat ISIS, deter North Korea, dissuade Russia, constrain Iran, and engage China. The question now is how to do all this in the context of the United States' changing global partnerships. A new strategic approach is needed.

Three broad U.S. approaches merit consideration. The first is assertiveness, which implies a degree of unilateralism. The United States would seek to vigorously advance the liberal democratic market-oriented brand that is under fire in Europe, Asia, and the Middle East and challenge alternative models. It would take an uncompromising line with Russia, China, Iran, North Korea, and Salafi jihadists in these three regions of the world. This would risk pushing some of these potential adversaries closer together and would reject the more flexible approach suggested in Chapter Three. This approach would strongly support partner positions in controversies with potential adversaries. It would seek to enlist partners in each regional effort, but the United States would be prepared to take a leading role in each area if needed. Small coalitions of willing partners would be the likely result. Such an assertive approach is generally consistent with American exceptionalism and increased defense budgets.

The second option is collaborative engagement. This strategy would seek to shift more of the burden and the responsibility to U.S. partners around the globe. This would include insisting on larger defense contributions from NATO allies, constructing a more-robust security architecture in Asia, and strengthening ties with major powers in the Middle East. Military assistance to vulnerable states would increase significantly. Some of the load would be lifted from the United States, but partners would have an increased voice in regional policies that might conflict with U.S. interests.

The third general approach is retrenchment to allow greater focus on rebuilding U.S. domestic strength. This approach would allow for greater focus on rebuilding domestic strength. It would focus national security attention on a narrow number of vital interests where security threats are existential and retrench from regions where interests are less than vital. For example, the United States might concentrate on major power military threats to treaty allies in Europe and Asia while reducing commitments in the Middle East. This strategy would also seek greater accommodation with potential adversaries where possible.

None of these three approaches is ideal; they all have strengths and weaknesses and are constrained in various ways. Assertiveness provides the greatest independence of action for the United States. Under this approach, the United States would often act alone or with a small coalition. If the United States sought to retrench and abandon some of its current international responsibilities, it could also do that best by acting independently and not focusing as much on its partners. A collaborative approach would limit U.S. independent action to the extent that it would need to defend those partners and rely more on them to jointly meet global responsibilities.

Similarly, assertiveness would provide the best way to defend U.S. values globally because a collaborative approach would require some accommodation with partners who may have somewhat different values. However, since most U.S. partners share universal values and respect for the rule of law, the collaborative approach places a close second. Retrenchment is the least likely to advance U.S. values.

Harnessing the power of U.S. partners is a key strength of the collaborative approach. Given the complexity of today's international challenges, it takes a substantial coalition to solve them. Working in collaboration with many others provides added legitimacy and, if necessary, coercive power. U.S. partners will need to contribute a greater portion of the overall defense burden under this approach, and there are indications in Europe and Asia that—despite a slow pace—they intend to do so. Both an assertive approach and a retrenchment approach run risks with regard to enhancing partner contributions. An assertive approach would allow partners to continue to defer to U.S. capabilities and continue free-riding. U.S. retrenchment could stimulate greater partner defense spending, as it may have done in the 1970s, but it could also cause allies to accommodate adversaries to a greater degree.

A collaborative approach is also probably the best way to deter or dissuade further menacing behavior on the part of potential U.S. adversaries. Chapter Three elaborates on that growing threat. It is also the best way to convert them to a more rules-based approach. Confronting them with a combination of united allies and effective coercive measures is a greater deterrent than a more unilateral U.S. approach. Retrenchment in the face of a growing threat is unlikely to deter or persuade as effectively.

If the goal of U.S. foreign policy is to limit national security costs, to allow for a greater focus on restoring domestic strength, and to avoid military conflict, retrenchment may be the strongest option. The risk, however, is that U.S. neglect could create even more dangerous international circumstances. Collaboration is the second-best option for preserving U.S. strength, in light of domestic constraints that limit U.S. assertiveness.

Based on these criteria, collaborative security appears to be an imperfect but still optimal approach from a global perspective. It maximizes deterrence, maximizes burden sharing, and provides international cooperation to solve complex issues. It has one principal drawback, which is that it could limit U.S. freedom of action. It will also require the United States to stimulate its partners to share more of the defense burden, which many will resist. Retrenchment is the least competitive approach, with drawbacks including minimizing deterrence and defense of U.S. values.

In light of the regional security challenges, a collaborative approach also seems optimal. Given Russian behavior in Ukraine, maintaining NATO unity in Europe is critical. An overly assertive U.S. approach would be seen by some as provocative, could break Alliance unity, and would discourage greater burden-sharing. Any further U.S. retrenchment in Europe, on the other hand, would raise doubts about the commitment to common defense and might lead Moscow toward adventurism. In Asia, U.S. retrenchment would be seen as abandonment by partners and could spark either excessive concessions to China or nuclear proliferation to compensate for a reduced U.S. security commitment. This suggests some mix of a collaborative and assertive approach for Asia. In the Middle East, the United States has tried both an assertive and a more restrained approach during the past 15 years, and succeeded at neither. Rebuilding ties with traditional Sunni partners while seeking a more collaborative relationship with Iran may lead to a better policy balance.

Implementing steps to achieve a stronger collaborative approach will pose difficulties and create several contradictions, but many of those contradictions can be resolved. Steps might include

- maintaining partner confidence in U.S. defense commitments while making clear that simultaneous conflict in three theaters would stretch current U.S. military capabilities
- seeking opportunities for better relations with China and Iran in particular without undermining U.S. relations with Japan and traditional Sunni partners
- enhancing the military capacity and political will of European allies at a time when they are divided on threat perceptions and focused on the future of the European Union
- creating stronger alliance structures in Asia, including strengthening Japan's defensive capabilities without causing China to believe that it is being encircled or contained
- rebuilding ties with traditional Middle Eastern partners without embracing their domestic policies
- defeating ISIS using a large coalition, much of which is unwilling to fight

- building greater defense capacity and resilience in vulnerable nations on limited military assistance budgets
- strengthening trilateral relations among the United States, Europe, and Asia when partners are preoccupied with growing security challenges in their own regions.

Some of these steps are already under way. The United States has strengthened its defense commitments to Europe during the past year through Operation Atlantic Resolve, the European Reassurance Initiative, and the NATO Readiness Action Plan. It has done the same in Asia by agreeing to new defense guidelines with Japan and strengthening bilateral defense relations with South Korea, the Philippines, Singapore, and Vietnam. It has maintained freedom of navigation exercises in the South and East China seas. It retains troops in Afghanistan and has reintroduced some 3,500 advisers in Iraq. It has kept its defense budget as robust as possible given battles over sequestration. More deterrence measures are being planned. At the same time, it is clear from the most recent Quadrennial Defense Review that fighting two major theater conflicts simultaneously would create difficulties for operations in the second theater. This somewhat contradictory perspective on commitments and capabilities should alert partners that they need to contribute more to the common defense.

Improving U.S. relationships with China and Iran could significantly shift the geostrategic environment back to the U.S. advantage. Relations with those two countries are troubled in large measure because the United States seeks to protect its regional partners from being harmed by them. So improving relations would need to be managed in a way that does not undermine those partners. In the case of China, the United States would need to help design a process to settle contending maritime claims before they erupt into major conflict. That process would need to be seen as transparent and fair by its Asian partners. The case of Iran is proving to be more difficult. If the United States can reach final agreement with Iran on the nuclear issue, it may need to provide military assistance offsets to assure the security of those Middle East partners that are skeptical about the results of those negotiations.

The United States' European allies now spend roughly one-half of what the United States spends on defense. At the September 2014 NATO Summit in Wales, they agreed to address this imbalance, and those with the lowest defense budgets agreed to increase them to 2 percent of GDP by 2025. The progress will be slow and some slippage is already evident. Chapter Five suggests multiple ways in which the United States might enhance Europe's defense capabilities, including getting Germany to agree to a specific plan to attain the 2-percent goal. A review of six decades of burden-sharing problems shows that only in the 1970s did the Europeans significantly increase their portion of NATO defense spending. That may have been the result of an enhanced threat perception, concern about U.S. retrenchment, a healthy European economy, and U.S. troop-withdrawal threats. Some have suggested that troop-withdrawal threats today could stimulate European defense spending. The problem is that the United States had some 350,000 troops in Europe in the 1970s, while today there are only some 65,000 deployed to deter an increasingly aggressive Russia. Many defense analysts are in fact considering ways to increase U.S. forward deployment in Europe. Alternative means will need to be found to give European allies a wakeup call.

Strengthening security architectures in Asia will require developing closer multilateral military cooperation among Japan, Australia, South Korea, and the ASEAN nations. Some of these ties are being reinforced in response to Chinese behavior in the South China Sea. This may inevitably lead China to conclude that it is being encircled by the United States and its partners in Asia. It remains to be seen whether China will respond with more belligerent policies or with compromise on maritime issues. A U.S. diplomatic initiative on South China Sea issues might steer China in the right direction.

The United States may wish to reinforce its relationship with several traditional Middle Eastern partners where differences over domestic policies have frayed ties in the past half-decade. Strengthening U.S. ties with Israel, Egypt, Saudi Arabia, and Pakistan will require the United States to overlook past differences and focus instead on mutual interests in regional stability. Given the difficulties that the United States will have in defeating ISIS without substantial ground forces, it will need to rely on several traditional pillars in the Middle East to avoid further spread of sectarian strife and terrorism. Reinforcing these traditional ties while seeking a new relationship with Iran will be a difficult diplomatic task. However, for decades, the United States was able to contribute to peace in the Middle East by maintaining close ties with both Israel and its Arab neighbors. Perhaps by creating stronger U.S. links with leading Sunni and Shi'a states, it can help to contain region-wide sectarian strife.

To reassure vulnerable partners, the United States and its more capable partners need to develop robust programs to enhance both defense capabilities and societal resilience in these vulnerable states. This is not an activity that the United States can conduct alone. Its stronger allies in both Europe and Asia need to increase their contributions to such efforts.

Finally, the United States should create new trilateral efforts to draw together its partners in both Europe and Asia that face similar security, political, economic, societal, and environmental problems. Trilateralism could in fact prove to be a good follow-on strategy to the pivot. Only by working together across regions can many of these challenges be effectively managed. The weak link is between European and Asian partners. The architecture for a new trilateralism might be called "variable geometry." The nations involved in each trilateral partnership could vary depending on the intended function. On the security front, the United States needs to develop closer interoperability among those countries to which it is bound by a common defense commitment. A next logical step would be to name both Japan and South Korea as NATO enhanced opportunity partners. On the economic front, completing both the TPP and TTIP trade negotiations is a crucial first step, to be followed by completion of EU free trade agreements with Japan and ASEAN nations. On the political front, an effort should be made to develop a trilateral forum that includes China. On the environmental front, the U.S.-China agreement limiting carbon emissions might serve as the basis for a new trilateral effort.

Taken together, these steps could serve as the basis for a more collaborative approach to U.S. national security strategy.

Abbreviations

A2/AD	anti-access/area denial
AIIB	Asian Infrastructure Investment Bank
ARF	ASEAN Regional Forum
ASEAN	Association of Southeast Asian Nations
CSBA	Center for Strategic and Budgetary Assessments
DPRK	Democratic People's Republic of Korea (North Korea)
EU	European Union
GDP	gross domestic product
IAEA	International Atomic Energy Agency
ICBM	intercontinental ballistic missile
IISS	International Institute for Strategic Studies
IMF	International Monetary Fund
ISAF	International Security Assistance Force
ISIS	Islamic State of Iraq and Syria
LNG	liquefied natural gas
MAP	Membership Action Plan
NATO	North Atlantic Treaty Organization

P5+1	China, France, Russia, United Kingdom, United States, and Germany
PLA	People's Liberation Army
RAP	Readiness Action Plan
RCEP	Regional Comprehensive Economic Partnership
ROK	Republic of Korea (South Korea)
TPP	Trans-Pacific Partnership
TTIP	Transatlantic Trade and Investment Partnership
UN	United Nations

References

Ackerman, Spencer, "Bullish Obama Vows to 'Degrade and Destroy' Islamic State," *The Guardian*, September 3, 2014.

Alderman, Liz, and Alison Smale, "Divisions Grow as a Downturn Rocks Europe," *New York Times*, August 29, 2014.

Allied Command Transformation, *Strategic Foresight Analysis*, North Atlantic Treaty Organization, April 8, 2013.

Allison, Graham, and Dimitri Simes, "Stumbling into War," *The National Interest*, May/June 2015.

"Al-Qaida/Al-Qaeda (The Base)," *GlobalSecurity.org*, updated May 21, 2015. As of October 7, 2015:
http://www.globalsecurity.org/military/world/para/al-qaida.htm

Applebaum, Anne, "Is It 1939 Again in Europe?" *Washington Post*, August 31, 2014.

———, "The End of Britain as We Know It," *Washington Post*, May 11, 2015.

"August 1985: Pressler Amendment Passed, Requiring Yearly Certification that Pakistan Does Not Have Nuclear Weapons," HistoryCommons.org, undated. As of September 10, 2015:
http://www.historycommons.org/context.jsp?item=a0885presslleramendment&scale=0#a0885presslleramendment

"Awkward Relations," *The Economist*, March 29, 2014. As of September 10, 2015:
http://www.economist.com/news/middle-east-and-africa/21599767-american-president-and-saudi-king-will-have-unusually-edgy

Bader, Jeffrey A., *Obama and China's Rise: An Insider's Account of America's Asia Strategy*, Washington, D.C.: Brookings Institution, 2012.

Barry, Charles, and Samuel Greene, "European Military Capabilities in the 21st Century," National Defense University working draft, January 2013.

de la Baume, Maïa, "French Defense Minister Says Russia May Never Receive Mistral Warships," *New York Times*, December 5, 2014.

Bell, Benjamin, "ISIS Intent on Hitting West, McCaul Believes," *ABC News*, August 24, 2014.

Bennhold, Kathrin, "A Chasm Divides Leaders of a Kingdom Still United," *New York Times*, May 11, 2015.

Bergen, Peter, "Why the Saudis Unfriended the U.S.," *CNN.com*, March 28, 2014. As of September 10, 2015:
http://www.cnn.com/2014/03/26/opinion/bergen-obama-saudi-tensions/

Binnendijk, Hans, ed., *A Transatlantic Pivot to Asia: Towards New Trilateral Partnerships*, Washington, D.C.: Center for Transatlantic Relations at Johns Hopkins University, School of Advanced International Studies, 2014a.

———, "The American Pivot and NATO Engagement in the Indo-Pacific Basin," Center for Transatlantic Relations, May 2014b.

———, "Conditions for the Iran Nuclear Deal," *Defense News*, August 16, 2015.

Binnendijk, Hans, Debra Cagan, and Andras Simonyi, "NATO Enlargement and Enhanced Partnership: The Nordic Case," in Daniel S. Hamilton, Andràs Simonyi, and Debra Cagan, eds., *Advancing U.S.-Nordic-Baltic Security Cooperation: Adapting Partners to a New Security Environment*, Washington, D.C.: Center for Transatlantic Relations at Johns Hopkins University, School of Advanced International Studies, 2014.

Binnendijk, Hans, and Alan Henrikson, *Back to Bipolarity?* Washington, D.C.: National Defense University, Strategic Forum No. 161, May 1999.

Birnbaum, Michael, "Chinese Leader Signs Trade Deals with Russia," *Washington Post*, October 14, 2014a.

———, "NATO Intercepts Several Russian Jets," *Washington Post*, October 30, 2014b.

Blackwill, Robert D., and Ashley J. Tellis, *Revising U.S. Grand Strategy Toward China*, Washington, D.C.: Council on Foreign Relations, Council Special Report No. 72, March 2015.

Blasko, Dennis J., "The 2015 Chinese Defense White Paper on Strategy in Perspective: Maritime Missions Require a Change in the PLA Mindset," *China Brief*, Vol. 15, No. 12, May 29, 2015.

Bonds, Timothy M., *Limiting Regret: Build the Army We Will Need*, testimony presented before the National Commission on the Future of the Army, August 18, 2015. As of September 1, 2015:
http://www.rand.org/pubs/testimonies/CT437.html

Bowie, Robert, "Nunn Amendment: NATO Must Do More on Conventional Arms," *Christian Science Monitor*, June 29, 1984.

Canadian Department of National Defence, *The Future Security Environment 2008–2030, Part 1: Current and Emerging Trends*, Ottawa, 2009.

Carter, Sara, "Pakistan Is No Ally of the U.S. and the 'Toxic' Relationship Threatens National Security: Former Pakistani Ambassador," *The Blaze*, December 2, 2013. As of September 10, 2015:
http://www.theblaze.com/stories/2013/12/02/pakistan-is-no-ally-of-the-u-s-and-the-toxic-relationship-threatens-national-security-former-pakistani-ambassador/

Castle, Stephen, "British Premier Urges Military to Spend More to Fight ISIS," *New York Times*, July 13, 2015.

"China, Russia Sign Accord on Second Gas Route," *Associated Press*, November 9, 2014.

Clingendael International Energy Programme, *Russian Gas Imports to Europe and Security of Supply*, fact sheet, undated. As of September 29, 2015:
http://www.clingendaelenergy.com/files.cfm?event=files.download&ui=9C1DEEC1-5254-00CF-FD03186604989704

Clinton, Hillary Rodham, "America's Pacific Century," *Foreign Policy*, October 11, 2011.

Colucci, Lamont, "Voters Want America to Lead," *U.S. News and World Report*, March 18, 2015.

Cooper, Helene, and Mark Landler, "U.S. Mobilizes Allies to Widen Assault on ISIS," *New York Times*, August 26, 2014.

Craig, Tim, "Pakistani Military Says It Achieved Major Victory in Mountain Assault," *Washington Post*, July 4, 2015.

Cronin, Patrick M., Richard Fontaine, Zachary M. Hosford, Oriana Skylar Mastro, Ely Ratner, and Alexander Sullivan, *The Emerging Power Web: The Rise of Bilateral Intra-Asian Security Ties*, Center for a New American Security, June 2013. As of September 9, 2015:
http://www.cnas.org/files/documents/publications/CNAS_AsiaPowerWeb.pdf

Delégation aux Affaires Stratégiques, *Strategic Horizons*, Paris: French Defense Ministry, 2013. As of August 20, 2015:
http://www.defense.gouv.fr/das/reflexion-strategique/prospective-de-defense/articles-prospective/strategic-horizons

Dempsey, Judy, "What Tusk and Mogherini Mean for Europe," *Strategic Europe* blog, Carnegie Europe, September 1, 2014. As of September 1, 2015:
http://carnegieeurope.eu/strategiceurope/?fa=56502

Dionne, E. J., Jr., "David Cameron's Wizardry," *Washington Post*, May 11, 2015.

Dobbins, James, Richard H. Solomon, Michael S. Chase, Ryan Henry, F. Stephen Larrabee, Robert J. Lempert, Andrew Liepman, Jeffrey Martini, David Ochmanek, and Howard J. Shatz, *Choices for America in a Turbulent World*, Santa Monica, Calif.: RAND Corporation, RR-1114-RC, 2015. As of September 10, 2015:
http://www.rand.org/pubs/research_reports/RR1114.html

Douthat, Ross, "Our Thoroughly Modern Enemies," *New York Times*, August 23, 2014.

Drake, Bruce, "More Americans Say U.S. Failed to Achieve Its Goals in Iraq," Pew Research Center, June 12, 2014. As of September 1, 2015:
http://www.pewresearch.org/fact-tank/2014/06/12/more-americans-say-us-failed-to-achieve-its-goals-in-iraq/

Erdbrink, Thomas, "Post-Deal Iran Asks If U.S. Is Still 'Great Satan,' or Something Less,'" *New York Times*, September 17, 2015.

European Commission, *Transatlantic Trade and Investment Partnership: The Economic Analysis Explained*, September 2013. As of September 29, 2015:
http://trade.ec.europa.eu/doclib/docs/2013/september/tradoc_151787.pdf

European Union Institute for Security Studies, *Global Trends 2030—Citizens in an Interconnected and Polycentric World*, Condé-sur-Noireau, France: Corlet Imprimeur, 2012.

Fifield, Anna, "Japan's Leader Stops Short of WWII Apology," *Washington Post*, August 14, 2015.

Fisher, Max, "American Isolationism Just Hit a 50-Year High. Why That Matters," *Washington Post*, December 4, 2015.

Freedman, Lawrence, *Strategy: A History*, New York: Oxford University Press, 2013.

Frumin, Aliyah, "Obama's Rocky Relationship with Israel: A Timeline," *MSNBC.com*, September 13, 2013. As of September 10, 2015:
http://www.msnbc.com/hardball/obamas-rocky-relationship-israel-tim

Gause, F. Gregory, III, *Beyond Sectarianism: The New Middle East Cold War*, Doha, Qatar: Brookings Doha Center, Analysis Paper No. 11, July 2014.

Goldman, Adam, "Officials: Islamic State Doesn't Pose an Immediate Danger to U.S.," *Washington Post*, September 11, 2014.

Gompert, David, and Hans Binnendijk, "Will Putin Fall Victim to One of History's Classic Blunders?" *The RAND Blog*, April 14, 2014a. As of September 29, 2015:
http://www.rand.org/blog/2014/04/will-putin-fall-victim-to-one-of-historys-classic-blunders.html

———, "The Power to Coerce," *U.S. News and World Report*, July 9, 2014b.

Gompert, David C., Hans Binnendijk, and Bonny Lin, *Blinders, Blunders and Wars: What America and China Can Learn*, Santa Monica, Calif.: RAND Corporation, RR-768-RC, 2014. As of August 20, 2015: http://www.rand.org/pubs/research_reports/RR768.html

Gul, Ayaz, "Olson: US-Pakistan Relations Still Challenging, Improving," *Voice of America*, February 3, 2014. As of September 10, 2015: http://www.voanews.com/content/us-pakistan-relations-still-challenging-improving/1843105.html

Hachigian, Nina, ed., *Debating China: The U.S.-China Relationship in Ten Conversations*, Oxford: Oxford University Press, 2014.

Hamilton, Daniel S., and Pedro Schwartz, *A Transatlantic Free Trade Area—A Boost to Economic Growth?* Brussels: New Direction, undated.

Hamilton, Daniel, and Kurt Volker, eds., *Transatlantic 2020: A Tale of Four Futures*, Washington, D.C.: Center for Transatlantic Relations, 2012.

Hammes, T. X., *Offshore Control: A Proposed Strategy for an Unlikely Conflict*, Washington, D.C.: National Defense University, Strategic Forum No. 278, June 2012.

Han, Stephanie, and Natalie Soraka, *U.S. Trade Overview, 2013*, Washington, D.C.: Department of Commerce, October 2014.

IISS—*See* International Institute for Strategic Studies.

International Institute for Strategic Studies, *The Military Balance 2012*, London, March 7, 2012.

———, *The Military Balance 2014*, London, February 5, 2014.

Isachenkov, Vladimir, "Russia Submits Revised Claim for Vast Arctic Seabed Territories at United Nations," *Associated Press*, August 4, 2015.

Jaffe, Greg, "Germany's Merkel Will Be Key to Obama's Success at G-7," *Washington Post*, June 8, 2015.

Jimin, Chen, "The Paradox of Abe's Speech," *Chinausfocus.com*, August 25, 2015. As of September 29, 2015: http://m.chinausfocus.com/article/3851.html

Joint Air Power Competence Center, *Present Paradox—Future Challenge*, Kalkar, Germany: North Atlantic Treaty Organization, March 2014a.

———, *Air and Space Power in NATO: Future Vector*—Part 1, Kalkar, Germany: North Atlantic Treaty Organization, July 2014b.

Joint Chiefs of Staff, *The National Military Strategy of the United States of America*, Washington, D.C., 2015.

Jones, Bruce, "Despite Growing Energy Independence, U.S. Cannot Escape Global Risks," *PlanetPolicy* blog, Brookings Institution, May 27, 2014. As of September 1, 2015:
http://www.brookings.edu/blogs/planetpolicy/posts/2014/05/27-energy-independence-us-global-risks-jones

Jones, Seth, "Islamic Jihadists: How Real a Threat?" *Christian Science Monitor*, March 30, 2015, pp. 26–32

Karnitschnig, Matthew, "German Businesses Urge Halt on Sanctions Against Russia," *Wall Street Journal*, May 1, 2014.

Keck, Zachary, "Russia Conducts Military Drill on Disputed Kuril Islands," *The Diplomat*, August 13, 2014.

Kelly, Terrence K., Anthony Atler, Todd Nichols, and Lloyd Thrall, *Employing Land-Based Anti-Ship Missiles in the Western Pacific*, Santa Monica, Calif.: RAND Corporation, TR-1321-A, 2013. As of September 9, 2015:
http://www.rand.org/pubs/technical_reports/TR1321.html

Kissinger, Henry, "Henry Kissinger on the Assembly of a New World Order," *Wall Street Journal*, August 29, 2014a.

Kissinger, Henry, *World Order*, New York: Penguin Press, September 2014b.

Korb, Lawrence, Max Hoffman, and Katherine Blakeley, "A User's Guide to the Fiscal Year 2015 Defense Budget," Center for American Progress, April 24, 2014. As of September 1, 2015:
https://www.americanprogress.org/issues/security/report/2014/04/24/88516/a-users-guide-to-the-fiscal-year-2015-defense-budget/

Kramer, Franklin D., *NATO Global Partners: Strategic Opportunities and Imperatives in a Globalized World*, Washington, D.C.: Atlantic Council, March 2013.

Lamothe, Dan, "U.S. General: North Korea Likely Can Build Miniaturized Nuclear Weapons," *Washington Post*, October 24, 2014.

Larrabee, F. Stephen, Stuart E. Johnson, John Gordon IV, Peter A. Wilson, Caroline Baxter, Deborah Lai, and Calin Trenkov-Wermuth, *NATO and the Challenges of Austerity*, Santa Monica, Calif.: RAND Corporation, MG-1196-OSD, 2012. As of September 3, 2015:
http://www.rand.org/pubs/monographs/MG1196.html

Lasconjarias, Guillaume, "NATO's Land Forces: Losing Ground," American Enterprise Institute, June 4, 2014. As of September 3, 2015:
http://www.aei.org/publication/natos-land-forces-losing-ground/

Layne, Christopher, *The Peace of Illusions: American Grand Strategy from 1940 to the Present*, Ithaca, N.Y.: Cornell University Press, 2006.

Lazar, Peter, *The Mansfield Amendments and the U.S. Commitment in Europe, 1966–1975*, thesis, Monterey, Calif.: Naval Postgraduate School, June 2003.

Lee, Grace, "The Political Philosophy of Juche," *Stanford Journal of East Asian Affairs*, Vol. 3, No. 1, Spring 2003.

Lindley-French, Julian, "China's Fiery Cross?" Lindley-French's Blog Blast: Speaking Truth unto Power, blog post, September 9, 2014. As of August 26, 2015: http://lindleyfrench.blogspot.com/2014_09_01_archive.html

Livingston, Robert Gerald, "Spies Get Between Germany and the United States," blog post, American Institute for Contemporary German Studies at Johns Hopkins University, July 15, 2014. As of September 3, 2015: http://www.aicgs.org/issue/spies-get-between-germany-and-the-united-states/

LoGiurato, Brett, "There's Been a Dramatic Shift in American Attitudes Toward Foreign Policy, and Hawks Think They Have Their Moment," *Business Insider*, September 10, 2014.

Mancinelli, Paul, "Conceptualizing 'New Type Great Power Relations': The Sino-Russian Model," *China Brief*, Vol. 14, No. 9, 2014.

Marquand, Robert, "Global 'Who's Who' of Asia Scholars Urge Japan to Own Up to WWII Atrocities," *Christian Science Monitor*, May 7, 2015. As of September 9, 2015:
http://www.csmonitor.com/World/Security-Watch/terrorism-security/2015/0507/Global-who-s-who-of-Asia-scholars-urge-Japan-to-own-up-to-WWII-atrocities

Mazarr, Michael J., "Land Power and a Third Offset through a Wide-Angle Lens," *Warontherocks.com*, June 21, 2015. As of September 1, 2015: http://warontherocks.com/2015/05/land-power-and-a-third-offset-through-a-wide-angle-lens/

Mazzetti, Mark, Michael S. Schmidt, and Ben Hubbard, "U.S. Suspects More Direct Threats Beyond ISIS," *New York Times*, September 20, 2014.

McCarthy, Justin, "Americans Split on Defense Spending," Gallup, February 20, 2015.

McDougall, Walter A., *Promised Land, Crusader State: The American Encounter with the World Since 1776*, Boston, Mass.: Houghton Mifflin, 1997.

McMorris-Santoro, Evan, "Obama Lays Out America's 'Core Interests' in the Middle East," *Buzzfeed News*, September 24, 2013. As of September 10, 2015: http://www.buzzfeed.com/evanmcsan/obama-lays-out-americas-core-interests-in-the-middle-east#.inEw1Ag2EN

Mearsheimer, John J., "Imperial by Design," *The National Interest*, No. 111, January/February 2011.

Merelli, Annalisa, "Home Abroad: These Are All the Countries Where the US Has a Military Presence," *Quartz*, April 2, 2015. As of September 1, 2015: http://qz.com/374138/these-are-all-the-countries-where-the-us-has-a-military-presence/

Merkel, Angela, "Remarks by Secretary Kerry: Remarks with German Chancellor Angela Merkel Before Their Meeting," Berlin, Germany, U.S. Department of State, October 22, 2014. As of August 20, 2015:
http://www.state.gov/secretary/remarks/2014/10/233242.htm

Miller, Greg, "New Rules for Visitors Exempt from Visas," *Washington Post*, November 4, 2014.

Minnick, Wendell, "China Threat: Air-Sea Battle vs. Offshore Control?" *Defense News*, June 23, 2014. As of September 9, 2015:
http://archive.defensenews.com/article/20140623/DEFREG03/306230019/China-Threat-Air-Sea-Battle-vs-Offshore-Control-

Modi, Narendra, and Barack Obama, "A Renewed U.S.–India Partnership for the 21st Century," *Washington Post*, September 30, 2014.

Nakamura, David, and Steven Mufson, "U.S. and China Announce Climate Deal," *Washington Post*, November 12, 2014.

NATO—*See* North Atlantic Treaty Organization.

Newport, Frank, "More Americans Now View Afghanistan War as a Mistake," Gallup, February 19, 2014. As of September 1, 2015:
http://www.gallup.com/poll/167471/americans-view-afghanistan-war-mistake.aspx

Norman, Laurence, and William Mauldin, "EU to Put New Sanctions on Russia," *Wall Street Journal*, September 11, 2014.

North Atlantic Treaty Organization, *Multiple Futures Project: Navigating Towards 2030*, 2009.

———, "Financial and Economic Data Relating to NATO Defence," press release, PR/CP(2014)028, February 24, 2014a. As of September 3, 2015:
http://www.nato.int/nato_static/assets/pdf/pdf_topics/20140224_140224-PR2014-028-Defence-exp.pdf

———, "NATO and Japan Conduct First Ever Joint Counter-Piracy Drill," web page, October 3, 2014b.

"North Korea Able to Miniaturize Nukes: DOD Intel Arm," *NTI Global Security Newswire*, April 12, 2013. As of August 26, 2015:
http://www.nti.org/gsn/article/nkorea-has-learned-how-miniaturize-nukes-dod-intel-arm/

"North Korea's Crimes Against Humanity Have 'No Parallel' Today," *Washington Post*, February 19, 2014.

Nuclear Threat Initiative, "Country Profiles: China," web page, updated July 2015. As of August 20, 2015:
http://www.nti.org/country-profiles/china/

Obama, Barack, "Text: Obama's Speech in Cairo," *New York Times*, June 4, 2009.

———, "Remarks by the President at the United States Military Academy Commencement Ceremony," West Point, N.Y.: The White House, Office of the Press Secretary, May 28, 2014. As of September 10, 2015: https://www.whitehouse.gov/the-press-office/2014/05/28/remarks-president-united-states-military-academy-commencement-ceremony

Ochmanek, David, *Sustaining U.S. Leadership in the Asia-Pacific Region: Why a Strategy of Direct Defense Against Antiaccess and Area Denial Threats Is Desirable and Feasible*, Santa Monica, Calif.: RAND Corporation, PE-142-OSD, 2015. As of September 9, 2015: http://www.rand.org/pubs/perspectives/PE142.html

Ochmanek, David, Andrew R. Hoehn, James T. Quinlivan, Seth G. Jones, and Edward L. Warner, *America's Security Deficit: Addressing the Imbalance Between Strategy and Resources in a Turbulent World*, Santa Monica, Calif.: RAND Corporation, RR-1223-RC, 2015. As of November 2, 2015: http://www.rand.org/pubs/research_reports/RR1223.html

Office of the Secretary of Defense, *Annual Report to the Congress on Military and Security Developments Involving the People's Republic of China*, Washington, D.C., 2013.

Office of the Under Secretary of Defense (Comptroller), *Department of Defense Fiscal Year 2016 Budget Request*, Washington, D.C., February 2015.

Pavel, Barry, and Magnus Nordenman, "Global Trends and the Future of NATO: Alliance Security in an Era of Global Competition," Washington, D.C.: Atlantic Council and Norweigan Institute for Defence Studies, October 2013. As of December 6, 2013: http://www.atlanticcouncil.org/images/publications/Global_Trends_and_the_Future_of_NATO.pdf

Payne, Sebastian, "What the 60-Plus Members of the Anti-Islamic State Coalition Are Doing," *Washington Post*, September 25, 2014.

Pew Research Center, "The New Sick Man of Europe: The European Union," web page, May 13, 2013a. As of September 1, 2015: http://www.pewglobal.org/2013/05/13/the-new-sick-man-of-europe-the-european-union/

———, *America's Global Image Remains More Positive than China's*, Pew Global Attitudes Project, July 18, 2013b. As of September 3, 2015: http://www.pewglobal.org/files/2013/07/Pew-Research-Global-Attitudes-Project-Balance-of-Power-Report-FINAL-July-18-2013.pdf

———, "Public Sees U.S. Power Declining as Support for Global Engagement Slips," web page, December 3, 2013c. As of September 29, 2015: http://www.people-press.org/2013/12/03/public-sees-u-s-power-declining-as-support-for-global-engagement-slips/

———, "Global Opposition to U.S. Surveillance and Drones, but Limited Harm to America's Image: Many in Asia Worry About Conflict with China," web page, July 14, 2014. As of August 26, 2015:
http://www.pewglobal.org/2014/07/14/global-opposition-to-u-s-surveillance-and-drones-but-limited-harm-to-americas-image/

Pew Research Center, "Obama Job Rating Ticks Higher, Views of Nation's Economy Turn More Positive," web page, January 14, 2015. As of October 5, 2015:
http://www.people-press.org/2015/01/14/obama-job-rating-ticks-higher-views-of-nations-economy-turn-more-positive/

Pollack, Jonathan, "Is Xi Jinping Rethinking Korean Unification?" briefing, Brookings, January 20, 2015. As of August 26, 2015:
http://www.brookings.edu/research/presentations/2015/01/20-xi-jinping-korean-unification-pollack

Posen, Barry R., *Restraint: A New Foundation for U.S. Grand Strategy*, Ithaca, N.Y.: Cornell University Press, 2014.

Preble, Christopher A., *The Power Problem*, Ithaca, N.Y.: Cornell University Press, 2009.

"Profile: Juche Idea," NorthKoreanChristians.com, undated.

Qazi, Shehzad H., "US-Pakistan Relations: Common and Clashing Interests," *World Affairs*, May/June 2012.

QinetiQ, Lloyd's Register, and the University of Strathclyde Glasgow, *Global Marine Trends 2030*, London, 2013.

Rapp-Hooper, Mira, and Bonnie Glaser, "In Confidence: Will We Know If US-China CMBs Are Working?" *Asia Maritime Transparency Initiative* blog post, Center for Strategic and International Studies, February 4, 2015. As of September 9, 2015:
http://amti.csis.org/in-confidence-will-we-know-if-us-china-cbms-are-working/

Raynova, Denitsa, and Ian Kearns, "Report: Six European Members of NATO Will Cut Defense Spending and Break Agreement Made at Wales Summit," *NATOSource* blog, The Atlantic Council, February 26, 2015. As of September 3, 2015:
http://www.atlanticcouncil.org/blogs/natosource/report-six-european-members-of-nato-will-cut-defense-spending-and-break-agreement-made-in-wales

"Russia and China Gang Up on U.S. Dollar as Economic Ties Deepen," *Moscow Times*, September 9, 2014.

Samuelson, Robert J., "Partners in Budget Posturing," *Washington Post*, March 30, 2015.

Sanger, David, "Obama Order Sped Up Wave of Cyberattacks Against Iran," *New York Times*, June 1, 2012.

———, "U.S. Confronts Consequences of Underestimating North Korean Leader," *Washington Post*, April 25, 2014.

Sang-Hun, Choe, "South Korean Leader Marks Anniversary of War's End with Warnings to North Korea," *New York Times*, August 15, 2015.

Saunders, Phillip C., *The Rebalance to Asia: U.S.-China Relations and Regional Security*, Washington, D.C.: National Defense University, Strategic Forum No. 281, August 2013.

Schmitt, Eric, "ISIS or Al Qaeda? American Officials Split Over Top Terror Threat," *New York Times*, August 4, 2015.

Schrayer, Liz, "Election Forecast: World Events Shake Isolationist Trends," blog post, U.S. Global Leadership Coalition, October 31, 2014. As of September 1, 2015:
http://www.usglc.org/2014/10/31/election-forecast-world-events-shake-isolationist-trends/

Sciutto, Jim, "Exclusive: China Warns U.S. Surveillance Plane," *CNN.com*, May 26, 2015. As of September 8, 2015:
http://www.cnn.com/2015/05/20/politics/south-china-sea-navy-flight/

Shanker, Tom, "Defense Secretary Warns NATO of 'Dim' Future," *New York Times*, June 10, 2011.

Sharp, Jeremy M., *Egypt: Background and U.S. Relations*, Washington, D.C.: Congressional Research Service, RL33003, June 5, 2014. As of September 10, 2015:
http://fpc.state.gov/documents/organization/227629.pdf

Shlapak, David A., "Towards a More Modest American Strategy," *Survival: Global Politics and Strategy*, Vol. 57, No. 2, 2015, pp. 59–78.

Shurkin, Michael, *Setting Priorities in the Age of Austerity: British, French, and German Experiences*, Santa Monica, Calif.: RAND Corporation, RR-222-A, 2013. As of September 3, 2015:
http://www.rand.org/pubs/research_reports/RR222.html

Simmons, Katie, Bruce Stokes, and Jacob Poushter, "NATO Publics Blame Russia for Ukrainian Crisis, but Reluctant to Provide Military Aid," Pew Research Center, June 10, 2015. As of September 3, 2015:
http://www.pewglobal.org/2015/06/10/nato-publics-blame-russia-for-ukrainian-crisis-but-reluctant-to-provide-military-aid/

Spiegel, Peter, "Putin Demands Reopening of EU Trade Pact with Ukraine," *Financial Times*, September 26, 2014.

Sreekumar, Arjun, "Which Country Relies Most Heavily On Russian Gas?" *USA Today*, August 31, 2014. As of September 29, 2015:
http://www.usatoday.com/story/money/business/2014/08/31/which-country-depends-most-heavily-on-russian-gas/14758961/

Stockholm International Peace Research Institute, "SIPRI Military Expenditure Database," spreadsheet data, undated. As of June 2015:
http://www.sipri.org/research/armaments/milex/milex_database

Swaine, Michael D., "Chinese Views and Commentary on the East China Sea Air Defense Identification Zone (ECS ADIZ)," *China Leadership Monitor*, No. 43, Spring 2014.

Swanson, Emily, "AP-NORC Poll: Terror Tops Americans' Foreign Policy Concerns," *Associated Press*, August 14, 2015.

Tatsumi, Yuki, "4 Takeaways from the New US-Japan Defense Guidelines," *The Diplomat*, April 29, 2015.

Thayer, Carlyle A., "South China Sea: A Commons for China Only?" *Yale Global* online, July 7, 2011. As of August 20, 2015:
http://yaleglobal.yale.edu/content/south-china-sea-commons-china-only

Thomas, Andrea, "Merkel Stresses Need to Prepare More Sanctions Against Russia," *Wall Street Journal*, September 1, 2014.

Tomlinson, Lucas, "'Stalemate': Size of ISIS Forces Unchanged Despite Year-Long Air Campaign," *FoxNews.com*, August 4, 2015. As of September 29, 2015:
http://www.foxnews.com/politics/2015/08/04/
one-year-later-concern-war-against-isis-at-stalemate/

UK Ministry of Defence, *Global Strategic Trends—Out to 2040*, 4th ed., London, 2010. As of August 20, 2015:
https://www.gov.uk/government/uploads/system/uploads/attachment_data/
file/33717/GST4_v9_Feb10.pdf

U.S. Department of Defense, *Sustaining U.S. Global Leadership: Priorities for 21st Century Defense*, Washington, D.C., January 2012.

———, "DOD Releases Estimated Impacts of Sequestration-Level Funding Report," news release NR-187-14, Washington, D.C., April 15, 2014a. As of September 1, 2015:
http://archive.defense.gov/Releases/Release.aspx?ReleaseID=16645

———, *Quadrennial Defense Review 2014*, Washington, D.C., 2014b.

U.S. Department of State, "U.S.-China Strategic and Economic Dialogue Outcomes of the Strategic Track," media note, Washington, D.C., June 24, 2015. As of August 26, 2015:
http://www.state.gov/r/pa/prs/ps/2015/06/244205.htm

U.S. Joint Forces Command, *Joint Operating Environment 2010*, Norfolk, Va.: U.S. Government Printing Office, 2010.

U.S. National Intelligence Council, *Global Trends 2030: Alternative Worlds*, Washington, D.C.: U.S. Government Printing Office, 2012.

Wasserbly, Daniel, "U.S. Military Views North Korea's ICBM as Operational," *IHS Jane's 360*, April 8, 2015.

Walt, Stephen M., *Taming America's Power: The Global Response to U.S. Primacy*, New York: W. W. Norton and Company, 2005.

Weisman, Jonathan, "In Letter, Obama Tells Congress U.S. Will Still Press Iran," *Washington Post*, August 21, 2015.

The White House, *National Security Strategy*, Washington, D.C., February 2015.

Whitlock, Craig, "Pentagon Expands Footprint in Africa," *Washington Post*, September 2, 2014.

Williams, Stuart, "Turkey Calls for Help with Syrian Refugees as Tensions Rise," *The Daily Star* (Lebanon), August 15, 2014.

Witte, Griff, and Dan Balt "Britain Faces Crucial Choices," *Washington Post*, May 10, 2015.

Yoshihara, Toshi, and James R. Holmes, "Thinking About the Unthinkable: Tokyo's Nuclear Option," *Naval War College Review*, Vol. 62, No. 3, Summer 2009, pp. 59–78. As of September 9, 2015:
https://www.usnwc.edu/getattachment/f1dc7a03-fab4-4a5b-9be2-f8c3e5baf430/Thinking-about-the-Unthinkable--Tokyo-s-Nuclear-Op

Yost, Casimir, "Out of the Quicksand," *The American Interest*, Vol. 9, No. 5, 2014. As of September 10, 2015:
http://www.the-american-interest.com/2014/04/09/out-of-the-quicksand/

Youssef, Nancy A., "Pentagon Fears It's Not Ready for a War with Putin," *The Daily Beast*, August 14, 2015. As of September 1, 2015:
http://www.thedailybeast.com/articles/2015/08/14/pentagon-fears-it-s-not-ready-for-a-war-with-putin.html